SO MUCH TO LEARN

(AND SO LITTLE TIME)

By
Aaron McAlexander

Third grade at the Meadows of Dan School, 1933.

Dedicated to Mrs. Eunice,
my first teacher,
and to Emra and Ian,
from whom I am still learning.

ISBN-13 978-0-9854225-1-6

Printed in U.S.A.

CONTENTS

Prologue

The schools ain't what they used to be and never was.

—Will Rogers

The morning of September 3, 2012, the day after Labor Day, seemed very strange to me. That was the first Tuesday after Labor Day in sixty seven years that I was not supposed to be somewhere in school in one capacity or another. I have to do something besides mow the lawn, so I plan on keeping myself busy by writing. This is a collection of tales about events experienced by me and by people I knew in school, near school, or while avoiding school. I guess you could say that I'm talking out of school.

Everyone has recollections of their school experiences, both good and bad, and some folks like to talk about them. Folks have been telling me for years about how education in America has been going downhill ever since they were in school. Just mention the word education, and they will be happy to tell you why they believe that to be the case.

To me, the public schools these days present a real conundrum. While I find much of what I see to be encouraging, I also feel that the students are not being sufficiently challenged in many cases. I do find it disturbing to observe high schools graduating kids who are unable to write in cursive or make simple mathematical calculations. Maybe they all have smart phone apps for all that sort of thing, but it is probably not a stretch to figure that the inability of folks to calculate basic stuff like interest payments and fuel mileage has contributed to our current economic problems.

I had been thinking about putting this collection of educational anecdotes, observations, and complaints together for some time, and in August of 2011, there came an early morning telephone call that got me seriously started on a project.

When I answered the telephone that morning, the caller did not begin with a greeting or an introduction of any kind. A voice from the phone just matter-of-factly announced, "The dang school burned down last night."

The announcement didn't register with me at first. I probably just responded with, "How's that again?" So the voice repeated, more emphatically this time, "The dang school burned down last night! The Meadows of Dan School, it's burned plumb down!"

I think I asked the caller, "Well, did it burn down to the ground? Is there anything left of it at all?" I was thinking about the walls being made of brick.

"The walls are still standing, but the roof fell in. There's really nothin' left. It's plumb gone," the caller assured me.

The caller did not identify himself, but I knew to whom I was talking. It was a friend of ours in Meadows of Dan, someone who will usually let us know if something important happens up there. But his farming keeps him awfully busy, so he doesn't waste a lot of time and words on telephone introductions and small talk. He usually just calls us, gives us the skinny, and signs off. That's it.

A few days later my wife and I drove up from Charlotte to see for ourselves, and everything was just like our friend said. A volunteer fireman in his younger years, our friend has seen enough to be able to judge if a burned building can be salvaged. Just as he said, the walls were mostly still standing, but the roof had fallen in. The floor of the second story had not collapsed, and through some of the missing windows, books stacked neatly on their shelves could be seen. They looked as though they could be pulled down and used at any time.

I have been told by people who know about construction that whenever the roof of a wood-framed building has collapsed, the structural integrity has been compromised. Even if the walls remain standing, the building cannot be salvaged. Like our friend said, "The school was plumb gone."

It had never occurred to me how I might feel if the Meadows of Dan school building no longer existed. I simply took its presence for granted; it had been there all my life and I guess I thought that it would be there forever. The United States Government *Works Progress Administration* (WPA) completed the neoclassical brick-veneered school building in the year I was born. It stood there as the stately center of the community throughout my school years and long beyond. I have now lived three-quarters of my life away from Meadows of Dan, but each time I returned, there the school building would be, looking much the same as it appeared the first time I walked through the big green doors at the age of four or five.

That building was more than just the structure where school children attended classes. A few generations ago, the school was the center of the community. Other than church services, most events which required space in which more than a few folks could congregate took place at the school.

I can't recall nearly all of the events my family and I attended at the school, but I can sure remember some of them. The school auditorium was the place where we practiced, played, and watched basketball games. It was the location of a number of musical shows, including performances by such famous names as Bill Monroe, Mac Wiseman, Jim Eanes, Arthur Smith, and many, many more. That auditorium was the place where I attended movies, auctions, talent shows, school plays, beauty pageants, graduation exercises, club meetings, and Halloween carnivals. My folks even dragged me to an Appalachian Electric Power appliance demonstration onetime. My favorite event was the Southern States Cooperative annual stock holders' meeting, where store owner Tom Agee personally distributed whole pints of ice cream to each person who came. Since everyone who bought a bag of Southern States cow feed or fertilizer from the Agee and Banks Store automatically became a stock holder, that took a lot of ice cream.

This was not the first Meadows of Dan School to have burned. The earliest school building that anyone now alive can remember burned down sometime around 1915. That fire, which was alleged to have been started deliberately, left the Meadows of Dan community without a real school building for several years. As result, many of the children four generations ago had to attend grade school across the line in Floyd County, many at either the Dickerson or the Stuart School. For a few years, some of the children attended a small, makeshift, one room school just a little way down the Mayberry Road from where the burned building had been. Anyone wanting to attend high school at that time had to go away to a boarding school such as Central Academy or Friends Mission.

The new four-room school building that was built at Meadows of Dan in the 1920's was intended to serve eleven grades. By the time it was replaced in 1939, it had become so crowded that some of the elementary grades were meeting across the road in the Baptist Church.

There were no desks in the church, so some first and second graders sat on the floor and used the front row pew seats as their desks. At about the same time, classes were also being taught in a defunct service station, a little asbestos sided building squeezed into the corner at the intersection of State Road 614 and US 58. That same building would later become the first incarnation of the Meadows of Dan "Tractor Place."

Some may wonder what the old school building near the Baptist Church looked like, but local folks over fifty have seen it and maybe even dined there. A part of the old wooden school building was moved down Highway 58 from its original site near the parkway and placed right next to the brand new school building. After some slight remodeling, it served as the school Cafeteria for about twenty-five years.

The Meadows of Dan School building, built by mostly local labor in the midst of the Great Depression, was reported to have cost something on the order $70,000.00. It stood there securely, with its old, pre-war electrical wiring for some seventy-two years. In the twenty-first century, a state-of-the-art gymnasium and elevator were added at a cost exceeding a million dollars. The old school building was then destroyed within a year by a faulty electrical connection. There has to be a lesson to be learned there somewhere. If our old school buildings won't last forever, than neither will we. I decided I had better get busy.

About a third of these tales have a direct connection to the Meadows of Dan School. Another third are about some experiences I had while preparing for a career in teaching, and the remainder are stories of events about which I was told or personally experienced while teaching. Some of the stories can be viewed as metaphorical, but I will let the reader decide which ones those are. The names of some of the people and places have been changed for reasons that should be obvious.

Education is what you get when you read the fine print. Experience is what you get when you don't.
— Pete Seeger

Lowering the Bar

Just recently, when another of our kin was being interred in the family cemetery, the workmen who dug the grave had to knock the boards off one section of the cemetery fence to give the backhoe access to the gravesite. They replaced the boards on the fence after the burial, but not without beating them up a bit. This prompted me to recommend that we replace a section of the fence with drawbars. When I made that suggestion, most of the family seemed to have no idea what I was talking about.

Now *drawbar* was a word in common use when I was a kid, and it meant about the same thing to everyone I knew. But it seems that the word has now taken on several new meanings and the old definition has all but disappeared.

One of the first tasks I can recall being given was opening drawbars, so that my dad could drive the car or the cows through the opening in the fence. This may not make a lot of sense unless one is familiar with the *old* meaning of *drawbar.* If you Google® *drawbar,* you are likely to find that it is a heavy metal bar used to connect an implement being towed to the vehicle doing the towing. You may already know that *drawbar* is another name for the cross bar on a three-point tractor hitch. But you may be amazed to learn that the stops on a vintage Hammond Organ are also called drawbars. I didn't know that until I Googled "drawbar!"

There is another important definition of drawbar: *Drawbar, n. A bar, or one of a set of bars, in a fence which can be drawn back or let down to allow passage, as along a road or a path.* That is the kind of drawbar I am talking about, a set of bars or rails across an opening in a fence. The rails can be slid all the way to one side of the opening to allow a vehicle to pass through. They can also be moved out of their supports at one end just enough to be dropped down, allowing livestock to move in or out. Surely, anyone who has passed the half-century mark and has rural roots can recall *drawbars*. Maybe some folks just always climbed over them to get to the other side of the fence.

Drawbars were constructed from whatever materials were at hand. The "bars" across the gap in the fence could be rough sawn boards or chestnut rails or trimmed saplings. Well-constructed drawbars had double posts at either side of the opening, with the bars supported by crosspieces nailed or wired to the twin posts. The ladder-like structure on each side made it easy to slide the bars or rails out of the way. Drawbars could sometimes be too easy to operate, given that cows and horses would sometimes learn to open them. (I am not kidding.)

I was about seven, I think, when I was informed that the opening of the drawbars was, from now on, going to be my responsibility. From that day forward, whenever my dad was driving along a country lane and came to a sudden stop, I understood that I would be the one to jump out of the car or off the wagon and pull down the drawbars. Once the bars had been moved completely to one side and out of the way of the vehicle, I would wait beside the gap in the fence until Dad had driven through. Often, he would then motion for me to slide the bars back across the opening. It was assumed that the drawbars being closed meant that there were livestock present somewhere.

Another feature common to many of the little mountain farms of a few generations ago was the milking gap. Any outdoor location where cows were routinely milked was called a milking gap, and it was normally located beside a fence and near a set of drawbars.

In the early summer, after our meadow had been mowed and the hay harvested, the cows would be allowed into the field to graze on the low growing clover that remained. The milking location would then be moved away from the barn. For the next several weeks, the milking was done beside the drawbars in the fence that separated the regular cow pasture from the meadow. The cows usually adapted to this change rather quickly, especially if they were regularly bribed with a scoop of cow chop. Being outdoors also had an advantage whenever a cow heeded the call of nature while being milked. Every herd had at least one cow that would withhold her bodily functions for the entire day, just waiting for the precise moment when someone would begin to milk her.

All this talk about drawbars has reminded me of an interesting story about a childhood friend of mine, who told it to me many years after we were in elementary school together.

When he was just a second grader, Willis was sent to live with his grandmother on a small mountain farm somewhat remote from the center of the community. The farm, like most in that time and place, had several fences with drawbars, with one of them the milking gap. Although his grandmother was getting along in years and could no longer manage the farm alone, she was not ready to completely give up farming. Willis was sent to help her out, and although he was a really well intentioned kid, he was rather young and not quite as much help as his grandmother expected at first.

Living on the farm with his grandmother had to be awfully lonely for Willis, especially in the summer when school was out. But he was a bright kid, and sometime in the summer before beginning the third grade, he discovered the Patrick County Bookmobile. Every two weeks during the summer vacation, when the bookmobile stopped at the Mayberry Store, Willis would be there to load up with a new stack of books. When he first discovered the bookmobile, Willis hadn't been reading for very long, but by the time he entered the third grade, people were calling him a bookworm.

Late in the third grade, his teacher told Grandmother Sally that Willis was reading several grade levels ahead of the third and retaining practically every word he read. There was not a lot at Grandma's house for him to read, but he quickly learned to use the school library, and neighbors began loaning him books and magazines. He read everything he could get his hands on, from Reader's Digest and the Bible, to The Farmers' Almanac and the Sears and Roebuck catalog. As soon as he got home from school every day, Willis would have his nose stuck in some kind of book.

The grandmother was proud of him doing so well in school, but she soon became concerned that he was spending too much time with his books. "Will," his grandmother would say, "get your nose out of that book right now and come help me with the milking. I need a little help around here. Besides, there's lots of things you need to learn about that you won't find in some ol' book."

Willis would reluctantly put down his book and grumble under his breath, grabbing up the milk buckets from the kitchen as he followed his grandmother out the back door. He did not mind the work so much, but he strongly disagreed with his grandmother's insistence that he would learn useful things from being outside and working on the farm. He did not accept the possibility that there was anything worthwhile that could not be found in a book. "Grandma, everything I am ever going to need to know, I can find somewhere in a book," he would argue. Then he would say to himself, "I don't plan to spend the rest of my life on this here farm."

When they got to the feed shed one evening, Willis slumped against the shed door while he waited for his grandmother to dip up a bucket of dry cow feed. "Will, take the buckets on up to the milking gap and let down the drawbars for the cows to come through. I'll be there in a minute," she instructed, and he obediently trudged up the hill.

A few minutes later, as Grandmother Sally followed, she was surprised to find Willis at the milking gap, still struggling with the drawbars. The cows were still on the other side of the fence and only the top two bars had been lowered.

Willis was making the very same mistake you might expect from someone who had never seen a drawbar. Anyone unfamiliar with opening drawbars will almost always begin at the top. But letting down the bars, beginning at the top, means that after the first bar is lowered, it is in the way of opening the second one down. Then, when both the first and the second bars are down, they will both be in the way of sliding out the third, and so on.

Grandmother Sally put her hands on her hips and watched with a mixture of disgust and amusement. She was tempted to let Will struggle a while longer, but it would soon be dark. She didn't just open the bars for him, though. She made him put the bars back up and then start again, this time beginning with the bottom bar and working his way up. In just a moment, the draw bars had been opened and the cows were coming through the fence.

After they had finished milking the cows and were carrying the milk to the springhouse, the grandmother had to give Willis a little talking-to about his difficulty with the drawbars. She even got a little sarcastic, something that was normally not a part of her nature.

"I can't rightly remember where I learned how to open drawbars," she told him. "I think maybe my mammy showed me how. I guess you think there's somewhere in a book where it says that when you open up drawbars, you start with the bottom one and work your way up to the top, instead of the other way around. When you find that in one of those books of yours, I want you to be sure and show it to me."

Singing Wheels, 4th Reader, Row Peterson, 1940

One can gain knowledge by reading,
but to gain wisdom, one must observe.
— Marilyn Vos Savant

Crossings

When was the last time you saw a chicken cross the road? That's what I thought. If you are an urban dweller and under fifty, you may have never, ever, actually seen a chicken cross the road. (The unfortunate creatures which have escaped from the crates on the trucks transporting them and become squashed on the interstate do not count.) I, however, am old enough and of rural enough origin that I do happen to know a thing or two about chickens crossing roads.

The chicken-crossing-the-road jokes do endure, and some of them remain modestly funny for some reason. Historically, "Why did the chicken cross the road?" is one of the oldest jokes around, with its first documented appearance in print going back to an 1847 edition of a New York City monthly magazine, *The Knickerbocker.* (Now what do people in NYC know about chickens crossing roads? One must assume that a hundred and sixty years ago, things were somewhat different in the Big Apple.)

I had always thought that the riddle was originated by Aesop, until I learned that the ancient Greeks did not have roads, only seaports. There is really nothing very funny about "Why did the chicken cross the Aegean?"

Until not too many years ago, chickens attempting to cross roads, sometimes unsuccessfully, were a commonplace distraction for travelers. This problem was doubtlessly exacerbated by the introduction of the automobile, but it must have been an everyday occurrence even when there were only animal

powered conveyances. Remember, the joke predates the automobile by at least sixty years.

The original response to the rhetorical question regarding the chicken's crossing was the not very funny "to get to
the other side." However, this original version laid (no pun
intended) the groundwork for a myriad of variations, including
the much funnier response, "To prove to the opossum that it is
possible." Even modern urbanites are familiar with the opossum's dismal road-crossing record.

In pre-World War II rural America, almost everyone
kept chickens. As chickens are prone to wander and practically
all chickens were free-range in those days, their travels would
occasionally take them to the other side of the road. In the time
and place of my childhood, the chicken crossing the road was
not merely the source of a riddle, but an occurrence which had
some real significance. A daytime drive in any direction from
my home was almost certain to be slowed by chickens crossing the road. These were not just any old anonymous birds that
happened to be crossing the road either. Most of them had iden-
tities. They would be either Posie Shelor's Leghorns, or Sally
Spangler's Dominiquers, or Coy Yeatts's Bald-Headed Shang-
hais. If a chicken was crossing the road anywhere within half a
mile of where it belonged, we knew the probable owner of the
chicken. And if a chicken was identified as crossing an inordi-
nate distance from where it was thought to belong, the crossing was sure to stimulate an expression of curiosity concerning
what that chicken was doing so far from its rightful domain.

Much of the interest regarding chickens' road crossing

in the past was due to the fact that it was not a simple, predictable act. In the days when the fowl ran free, there were
innumerable styles and techniques of road crossing, and they
depended upon many factors, including the breed of bird, the
motivation for the crossing, and the terrain bordering the road.
Chickens crossed the road for many reasons and their behavior while crossing thoroughfares was completely different from
that exhibited while crossing country lanes. Many of the road-
crossing styles were consistent and identifiable enough to be
given descriptive names. For example:

There was the *Dominiquer Stroll*, in which the chicken
engaged in the crossing was in no hurry at all, but sauntered
blithely across the road, apparently unaware there was an automobile anywhere in the vicinity. She would just doddle across
the road, scratching here and pecking there, accompanying her
stroll with a calm "arrrk, arrrk, arrrk" emitted in rhythm with a
rocking motion of her head.

In complete contrast to the Dominiquer Stroll was the
Squawking Fly-by. This was a crossing technique in which a
chicken would burst from the weeds on one side of the road and
half run/half fly, squawking and flapping, completely across the
road, well in advance of the approaching vehicle and quickly
disappearing into the vegetation on the other side. Unless another car was simultaneous approaching from the other direction, this method was almost always successful. This was the
technique preferred by most of the smaller, lighter breeds such
as Leghorns.

The *Panicked Adjustment* was a method quite common

among Plymouth Rocks of both the white and red varieties. In this style of crossing, the chicken, upon reaching the center of the road, would suddenly decide that she did not want to cross after all and would pirouette into a panicked reversal of her path. Also known as the squirrel crossing technique, it was probably the style of crossing with the highest mortality rate. It obviously is the source of the question, "Why did the chicken go halfway across the road?" Answer: "She wanted to lay it on the line."

Occasionally a hen would abruptly burst from the weeds onto the road pursued from a short distance by a rooster with obvious amorous intent. We won't go there, except to report that in this style of crossing, with the rooster being so intently focused on the chicken of his dreams, he would meet with disaster far more often than did the hen. (There are certain obvious parallels that can be drawn between chicken and human behavior.)

Dumb as they may appear to the casual observer, chickens have successfully adapted to changing conditions. As the nation became interlaced with a network of paved roads, those birds reared near a busy highway soon learned to either time their crossings more carefully or to avoid the highway altogether. Those reared near a seldom used dirt pathway, however, continued to consider the road an appropriate locale for scratching, resting, and even nesting. The most spectacular crossings I can recall occurred when we were traveling on some obscure unpaved road, presumably while we were on the way to visit some distant relatives.

The chickens we encountered on these lightly-traveled trails acted as though they had never seen an automobile, and that may have actually been the case for some of the young pullets. As we would ease around a curve on a remote cow path and unexpectedly encounter a cluster of chickens scratching in the road, the group would abruptly explode, with fowl radiating from the center of the flock in all directions. Then, as things began to settle down following the initial explosion, every bird would simultaneously decide that she was on the wrong side of the road and must re-cross to the correct location immediately. That is, with the predictable exception of the one or two that would decide that their only possible avenue of escape was to run down the middle of the road in front of the car for the next quarter mile. We called that behavior "chickens crossing the road lengthwise."

With all these digressions, I still have not explained why, among citizens of a modern world, one in which a chicken crossing a road is a seldom seen phenomenon, do references to "the chicken crossing the road" continue to be found so apt and so humorous. My own explanation is that the "Why the crossing of the road riddle" continues to be applicable to many human endeavors, including politics, religion, literature, science, and philosophy. Allow me to demonstrate my case by example.

QUESTION: "Why did the chicken cross the road?"

ANSWERS: Plato: "For the greater good."

Chaucer: "So priketh hem nature in hir corages."

Emily Dickinson: "Because it could not stop for death."

Captain Kirk: "To boldly go where no chicken has gone before."

John Calvin: "It was predestined as a part of the Almighty's perfect plan."

Albert Einstein: "Whether the chicken was crossing the road or the road was sliding under the chicken depends upon your frame of reference."

Bill Clinton: "It depends on your definition of 'cross.' "

George W. Bush: "Well, uh, the chicken, decided to cross the road because she was, uh, the decider."

Dick Cheney: "Where's my gun?"

Barack Obama: "Because it can."

We cannot leave this discussion without paying homage to some of the many modern derivatives in which something other than a chicken crosses the road. For example:

"Why did the dinosaur cross the road?" Answer: "Because it had not yet evolved into a chicken."

Or, "Why did the chewing gum cross the road"? The answer is, obviously, "Because it is stuck on the chicken's foot."

If at first you don't succeed, try, try again. Then quit. There's no point in being a damn fool about it.

—W. C. Fields

A Rare Bird Indeed

In the early years of the Great Depression, most of the children in these Blue Ridge Mountains were attending little one and two room schools that bore the same names as their mountain communities. There was the Meadows of Dan School, the Bent School, Free Union, Bell Spur, Mayberry, and Mountain View, to name just a few.

In 1928, when Miss Eunice first began her teaching career in the two-room Mayberry School, many of the students were still practicing their writing and arithmetic using soapstone pencils to scribe on stone slates. For most of the students, notebook paper, even the really basic kind that sometimes had wood splinters in it, was a luxury. A few of the students wrote their letters and ciphers on factory-made store-brought ceramic slates, but most used writing slates that were much heavier and rougher. Many of these were made from slabs of flagstone that were quarried locally, dressed, framed, and donated to the school by the local tanner, Simon Scott.

In our schools of the twenty-first century, many teachers would not know how to begin instructing a class without the availability of several forms of instructional media and audio-visual aids. In the 1930's, though, terms such as instructional media and audio-visual aids were largely unknown, even to professional educators. The Mayberry School was not so far behind the times as one might suppose. There actually were a few instructional aids in use there, although some of them were admittedly makeshift.

There was a set of large black cards, boldly printed with the English alphabet in white letters, pinned to the wall above the blackboard of the classroom used for grades 1-3. The set of cards included both upper-case and lower-case letters, in both Roman print and cursive writing. Most of the students at the Mayberry School were able to write in cursive by the time they finished the second grade, but they would occasionally need to check the cards above the board to confirm how a letter should be formed. I have had friends from the Mayberry area show me letters and documents written by their parents or grandparents, pointing out with pride the beautiful cursive handwriting of their ancestor. "Just look at that wonderful, even handwriting," they might say. "Can you believe that my grandmother only went through the fifth grade at Mayberry?"

The Mayberry School was fortunate to be in possession of a complete, though well-worn, set of full-color human anatomy charts. The charts, mounted on a rickety metal tripod, had been donated to the school when the local doctor had closed his medical practice years before.

The story was told of one small child, who upon entering his classroom for the first time, marched up to the front and examined the anatomy chart. The chart happened to be turned to a display of the interior of the human abdomen. The youngster immediately pointed to the intestines revealed in the cut-a-way view and loudly announced to everyone in the room, "Lookey there! Them there is hog guts!"

Another AV-aid, as it would be called today, was Miss Eunice's box of colored chalk. She ordered her set of eight bright chalk colors from Binny-Smith and Co. and paid for it personally, out of her monthly salary of $30.00.

It is too much to expect that any teacher will be beloved by all of his or her students, but Miss Eunice was very well-liked by most. Anyone could see that she cared about them all so very much. A large part of the love shown for her by the students was in return for the love she had for every one of them. Shy or boisterous, pretty or plain, weak or strong, she loved them all, and they all knew it. Kids can tell about things like that.

When she began teaching at the Mayberry School at the age of nineteen, Eunice Yeatts became the third of Edna and Dump Yeatts' daughters to teach there. The Mayberry School usually had two or three teachers, and when one of the older Yeatts sisters, Miss Della, left for greener pastures in Colorado, Miss Eunice took her place at the Mayberry School. Later, when Miss Lora Yeatts followed her older sister to Colorado (they may have been looking for potential husbands, to whom they would not be kin), a fourth Yeatts sister took over from her older sibling at the Mayberry School. With so many of the teachers in the school having the same last name, it avoided a lot of confusion to just call them Miss Della, Miss Lora, etc. rather than calling all of them *Miss Yeatts*.

It was no coincidence that the teachers at the Mayberry School were all called "Miss." Like many school systems in those days, Patrick County would not hire married women as teachers. (Rules like these were obviously the source of the stereotype of the old-maid school teacher.) Fortunately, by the time Miss Eunice got married and changed her last name, five years had passed, the policy had been changed, and she was allowed to keep her job. Even with the change in her last name, the students could see no good reason to alter what they called their teacher. This was long before the introduction of the status-neutral title of *Ms.,* so she was addressed by the phonic version of her title for the remaining thirty-seven years of her career. Whether the students meant to call her Miss Eunice or Mrs. Eunice, inside the classroom and out, she was always addressed as "Miz Eunice."

Miz Eunice and her sisters were all somewhat musically and artistically talented, which was definitely a benefit to the schools where they taught. For many years, from the 1920's into the 60's, it was standard procedure in elementary schools for the teachers to begin each school day with a fifteen or twenty minute "enrichment" time. Today, that period of time would be called "homeroom," and then as now, it was the time for the teacher to make school announcements and take care of logistics. But the teacher might also lead the students in singing, if she was musical, or encourage individual students to lead or to perform for the class if he or she was not. A teacher might choose to read to the students, possibly from a classic novel or from the Bible, a practice which was certainly not a problem for anyone then. If something exciting had happened in the life of a student, or if someone had some community news, they might be encouraged to share the event with the class.

The enrichment period also served another, more practical, purpose. Most of the students walked to school back then, and many had a lot of chores to do at home. Depending on the season and the weather conditions, the arrival time of many could be pretty uncertain. Enrichment period helped keep many of the students from missing so much of their early morning lessons and it could serve as a reward for the students' getting to school on time.

Most of the teachers had their own particular enrichment rituals, and Miz Eunice was known for bringing new creative activities to this special time. Many of these were related to her effort to instill in the students an appreciation for nature. She taught them about the local trees, flowers, wildlife, etc., having the students identify plants and animals by their official common names, as well as what they might be called locally.

It was in this "nature series" that Miz Eunice was able to put her new visual-aid of colored chalk into effective use. She wanted to make her third through fifth grade students more aware of the variety and beauty of the local wild bird and wild flower population. Aware that many of the boys in the school had little interest in birds other than their being available as handy targets, Miz Eunice decided to begin with the birds.

Miz Eunice planned to use her colored chalk to draw an image of a common songbird on the blackboard one morning each week. The students would be encouraged to try and identify the kind of bird she was drawing, even as its image was being revealed. Miz Eunice helped insure the success of the series by practicing her renditions of the birds on the board in the evenings, after all of the students had gone home. Her effort was rewarded by an enthusiastic student participation in her "bird on the board" presentations.

As one might expect, some of the students would sometimes become overly enthusiastic in their effort to be the first to identify the bird their teacher was drawing. Miz Eunice, who had some pretty liberal ideas about education for the time, did not want to interfere in the debates unless they really became too vigorous. She even encouraged students to challenge other's identifications of a bird. The kids were allowed to call out what was wrong about another student's identification. A student might react to another's identification of a bird with observations of their own; "But a Tit-mouse has a top-knot!" or "Everybody knows that a Towhee has red eyes!" for example. This would be considered an effective teaching strategy even today.

In a small, rural school such as Mayberry, long before the days of social promotion, there were usually a wide range of student ages in the same room. There might even be boys in fourth and fifth grades who would soon be leaving the school for the farm, the sawmill, or the coal mine, seeking work that could provide their families with badly needed cash. Some of the boys, as they approached the manly age of fourteen, had little use for academics. Miz Eunice was pretty good at keeping her students occupied with some creative learning task most of the time, but the contempt that some of them felt for "book-learning" would always be finding ways of expressing itself.

Shortly after school began one morning, Miz Eunice began the creation of an amazing, two-foot-high rendition of a common bird on the board. Well before the drawing was far enough along for a serious identification to be made, how ever, a bit of a ruckus erupted near the back of the room. The disagreement appeared to be between Ralph, a bright-but-lazy fourteen year-old, and young Alan, a serious and hard-working third grader. They already had a strong difference of opinion about the identity of the bird being drawn. Their conversation, though, was pretty basic.

"Tis."

"Tain't."

"Tis so."

"Tain't neither. Hit ain't no such a thing!"

As the volume of the disagreement escalated, Miz Eunice was forced to intervene. "What seems to be the matter back there?" She called out. "Alan?"

"Miz Eunice, that-there bird you're a-drawin' ain't what Ralph says it is, is it?

"Well, I don't know, Alan. What kind of bird does Ralph say that it is?"

"Ralph says that-there bird is a *Nekked-Assed Jay Bird,* and hit ain't so no such a-thing, is it?"

Miz Eunice caught her breath and nearly choked, turning quickly toward the board to hide her face and conceal the fact that she was struggling mightily to keep from bursting out loud with laughter. Finally, she regained enough control that she could turn back to the class and respond as any truly professional educator would – by converting the situation into a teaching moment.

"Indeed it is not!" she responded to Alan's question with a most serious expression on her face. "One should say that the bird is *not any such a thing*, or one can say that *it is no such a thing*. But Alan, one should never say that *hit ain't no such a-thing*. Then she added, just as a little joke of her own, "even when it ain't."

It isn't what we don't know that gives us trouble,
it's what we know that ain't so.

— Will Rogers

The Duel

Some of us mountain kids were just born with a rebellious streak to begin with. And some of the parents, unfortunately, harbored a less-than-enthusiastic attitude toward education in general and the new consolidated school in particular. This combination of influences made the maintenance of discipline at Meadows of Dan School a continuing challenge. But most of the time, the concerted efforts of the principal, the teachers, and the bus drivers kept order at a level where education could proceed mostly unimpeded. But this was only until the day that the school received an infusion of unparalleled defiance and insubordination, all in the personage of one determined, and apparently very unhappy, small boy.

It might have been his name that made him so mean. Or maybe his folks just didn't give him a name until he got old enough for them to see what he was going to be like. Duel (that really was his name) ended up in our school when he was placed in the home of an older couple in the Mayberry Community as a foster child. "He's just an unfortunate kid in unfamiliar surroundings. Right now, he is feeling lost and unloved," was my mom's compassionate opinion. Some of the teachers at the Meadows of Dan School held a less charitable opinion.

I was about halfway through the second grade when Duel first showed up, but he was initially placed in the third grade. After a few weeks, he was sent down to the second grade, placed under the no-nonsense tutelage of Miss Fain. This did not occur for any academic reasons, but simply because the third grade teacher informed the principal that one of them, either she or Duel, was going to be leaving the third grade right away.

Over sixty years later I can clearly recall him swaggering down the hall in our school. He looked bigger than he actually was. He had these really broad shoulders, and he leaned forward and rolled them when he walked, like he was pushing his way through a crowd. He walked that way even when the hall was empty.

Our principal, Mr. Knobloch, was a pudgy, well-educated man, who wore horned rimmed glasses and appeared to map his life along the route of minimum physical effort. He was an experienced educator, and although he took an instant dislike to Duel, he was determined to use an enlightened approach in managing one whom he thought might simply be misguided. Mr. Knobloch's dislike of Duel was more than fully reciprocated. Duel shrugged off the principal's stern lectures and disdainfully referred to his having to sit in the principal's office during recess as "nap time." Eventually, the punishments escalated to some rather mild applications of Mr. Knobloch's giant paddle, constructed in the theory that its appearance alone would be a major deterrent to any misbehavior. Duel declared himself immune to pain and continued about the business of standing every behavioral convention of the school on its head. Never have I known anyone so aptly named, for confrontation was the air Duel breathed. Although he may have succeeded in learning little in the classroom, he made a concentrated study of all the possible ways that could be found to disrupt the educational process and infuriate Mr. Knobloch. Apparently, there was also a couple of high school students from Mayberry who were constantly providing Duel with new ideas about ways he might antagonize Mr. Knobloch.

Duel was the only kid I knew in the second grade who frequently smoked, and I can't recall another elementary student ever bringing a jar of moonshine to school. He not only brought it, but had already consumed a large portion before the offense was uncovered. Unfortunately, the moonshine was discovered only after Duel began walking oddly and then threw up on the classroom floor. Duel claimed that he had the flu and that he had the jar of moonshine in his possession strictly for medicinal purposes.

Mr. Knobloch bought none of this explanation. After Duel had recovered from the "flu," the principal put his giant paddle to the test by giving Duel a lengthy and energetic walloping. The school secretary, who always witnessed such executions of justice, declared that she was concerned that Mr. Knobloch, being one so obviously in poor physical condition, might have a heart attack.

The application of more severe punishment to Duel did not have quite the result that Mr. Knobloch anticipated. While it may have been true that Duel became less confrontational with his behavior, he more than compensated with stealth. And while the number of trespasses which could be directly traced to Duel may have decreased somewhat, it was mostly because he had been able to recruit a group of assistants who were willing to take up any slack. One of Duel's new recruits was my own cousin, Jimmy. I remember Jimmy as being mostly a nice, quiet kid, who was very tall and strong for his age, but he didn't like school very much and he didn't like Mr. Knobloch a lot. By becoming a disciple of Duel, he gained an outlet for these feelings and gained an even stronger motivation to play hooky and go fishing.

Mr. Knobloch's response to the increase in the number of adversaries he faced was simple. Whenever either Duel or any of his disciples were caught in an offense, the principal applied a terrific walloping to Duel, often one completely out of proportion to the seriousness of the violation. And if the instigator of a transgression was unidentifiable, Mr. Knobloch automatically assumed that the chief culprit was Duel. It was soon obvious that these methods were not working, but it was equally clear, to students and teachers alike, that this was an irrational war and that Duel and Mr. Knobloch were locked in a mortal struggle for the soul of the school. Just about everyone was wondering how a contest of wills between two such determined antagonists might end, when, one fine April day, the escalating animosity reached its peak, and the conflict ended in a way that exceeded all of our expectations.

The ride from Mayberry to the Meadows of Dan School on this particular spring day was pretty routine until the bus was "on its way in," and about three miles from the school. Shortly after passing the Mayberry Presbyterian Church, the bus encountered a skunk in the road. The bus squashed the poor creature flat, but this animal was not your ordinary, everyday woods kitty. According to those riding the bus that day, it surely must have been the biggest and most powerfully equipped pole cat ever encountered in these parts. For the occupants of the bus, things were initially pretty unpleasant, but the accident was at least a diversion from the usual dreary bus ride to school. The otherwise unpleasant remainder of the trip to school was enlivened by a joyous exchange of accusations regarding the identity of the persons who might be responsible for such incredible flatulence.

Shortly after running over the skunk, as the bus stopped to pick up some more kids, Duel and Jimmy jumped off through the bus's back emergency door. There was nothing remarkable about that; they frequently abandoned the bus to go fishing or play hooky or to walk back to the store to buy cigarettes. Some of the students suggested that maybe the bus was near the area where Duel had previously found some stashed moonshine, and he and Jimmy were going to search there again. Anyway, the absence of Duel for the remainder of the bus trip to school was a little respite from fear for some of the younger riders.

By the time the Mayberry Bus got to school, most of its passengers could no longer smell the skunk odor so strongly. But, when that bus pulled up in front of the school, the kids who were outside the school playing, greeted it by holding their noses and yelling "Pee-yew! What happened to you?" Of course, to the riders of the Mayberry bus, that was really funny.

We were having math class, as I recall, and the teacher was turned away from the door and writing on the board, when Jimmy came quietly creeping into the classroom. Although he acted completely nonchalant as he took his seat, everyone else

in the room immediately realized that something very unpleasant had arrived with Jimmy.

"What on earth is that awful smell?" the teacher inquired, as she turned back to face the class.

"I, I think its Jimmy," Betty Lou, the girl sitting nearest
to Jimmy responded.

Before Miz Polly, our teacher, could confirm the source
of the smell within the room, there came a loud knock at the
classroom door. When the teacher opened the door, the pun-
gent wave that blew in from the hall was sufficient to send her
reeling. The assistant principal at the door announced that we
would all have to leave the building until the source of the odor
had been removed! Our classroom was way at the end of the
hall from the principal's office, but as we filed out of the building, it became obvious that the scent was coming from somewhere near there. As we milled around with the students from
the other classes, outside and upwind from the school building,
rumors of what had just happened began to circulate.

It seems that when Duel and Jimmy jumped off the Mayberry bus that morning, hooky was not what they had in mind.
Instead, they had walked back to the site where the skunk had
met its end and actually retrieved the mangled carcass from the
road. They picked it up, bare handed, and carried it the full
distance to the school. Jimmy told us later that, as they started
back to school with the dead skunk, one of them would carry it
by the tail until he was about to upchuck, and then the other one
would take over. "But you know," Jimmie told some of us later,
"after a while, we couldn't smell it at all. By the time I got to

school, I couldn't even tell that I was stinking."

Although Duel and Jimmy had alternated the duty of carrying the critter to the school, the whole caper was conceived by Duel, so he was given the honor of actually tossing the skunk into the principal's office.

The school secretary later described how she was sitting at her desk in the principal's office that morning, routinely checking the daily attendance reports. Mr. Knobloch, seated at his desk nearby, had just commented that they were going to have to send the Mayberry bus up to the Esso Station and get it washed, the skunk smell being so much worse than he first thought. This observation had barely been uttered, when a dead skunk, propelled by an unseen hand, came sailing in through the open office door and landed with a "plop" in the center of Mr. Knobloch's desk. The secretary testified that the effect was so intense that, while Mr. Knobloch ran out the front door of the office, bellowing that he knew who was responsible, she ran, gagging and choking, to open the window. It was from that window that she saw Duel casually sauntering down the walk and away from the front door of the school.

Although the culprits who delivered the skunk to the school and chucked it into the principal's office were not actually observed in the act, they were really not all that hard to identify. And they did not head for the tall timber to hide out, as one might expect, but they continued to hang around the school to enjoy the full effect of their accomplishment and presumably, to accept accolades from their fellow students. The culprits were certain, I'm sure, that the other students could not help but admire their bravery and determination, even as they were suffering from the side effects.

As soon as Jimmy and Duel were apprehended, A high school student who drove a pickup to school was recruited to transport them to their homes. They rode home in the back of the pickup, while the assistant principal accompanying them rode inside the cab with the driver. Both boys were immediately suspended from school, with more appropriate punishments to be determined later, after the principal had conferred with the superintendent and members of the school board.

The reaction to the episode by the students was truly a mixture of horror and admiration.   Many were dismayed that the sanctity of our school had been violated to such an extreme, but it is also true that Mr. Knobloch was not a very popular principal. And even those of us younger students who attended school in constant fear of the wrath of Duel knew that not all of his demons were of his own creation. Besides, who could help but admire the courage of those who would commit such an act, being full aware of the retribution which was sure to follow, punishment from which there would be no possibility of escape.

When one considers the tenacity and endurance which enabled two eleven-year-olds to retrieve an object so disgusting that it made ordinary mortals gag, some respect must surely be due. They carried that awful burden for miles, all for the momentary pleasure (and indelible commentary) of chucking it into the principal's office. One can only imagine the seething resentment fermenting in the hearts of those boys, and the anger vented in that act. But the rest of us had to cope with the unpleasant effects for several days. For years afterwards, a spell of damp weather would bring back faint reminisces of that day.

This time, Mr. Knobloch knew things had gone too far for him to handle them personally. There was a closed hearing held by the school board, and I assume that the outcome was why Duel never returned to the Meadows of Dan School. Some theorized that he was sent away to reform school, but no one could say for sure. The words "reform school" were considered so onerous in our community that they were only muttered in whispers. But it seemed logical to us kids, whatever it took for one to be sent there, this was an act which surely must qualify.

Whatever Duel's fate may have been, the proceedings appeared to have really made an impression on Jimmy. I imagine that the principal assured the board that the entire caper was inspired by Duel; no one seemed to doubt that it was conducted under Duel's leadership and that he was the one who actually threw the skunk into the office. Jimmy, assumed to be merely an accomplice, was allowed back in school after only a week of suspension and a Knobloch walloping. Jimmy quickly returned to being a fairly good kid. Years later, he would tell some of us that being walloped by the principal's giant paddle wasn't as scary as it seemed. "You know, Mr. Knobloch couldn't really paddle that hard," he claimed. "You could hardly feel it after the first lick."

That was Mr. Knobloch's last year as principal at the Meadows of Dan School. It was rumored that he had landed a position as principal of a much larger school somewhere in

North Carolina, and most folks figured that his moving on was the best thing for everyone. Most of us kids soon returned to what would be was considered within the range of normal behavior, putting an end to a most remarkable era in the history of our mountain school. I am confident that not one of us who was in attendance at Meadows of Dan School on that April day has forgotten Duel's grand finale'.

Many years later, while working as an educator myself, I ran into my old principal at a professional meeting. His name tag said "Dr. Fredrick Knobloch," and I recognized him immediately. When I introduced myself and I told him that I had been a student at the Meadows of Dan School while he was principal there, he grabbed my hand and shook it vigorously, greeting me like some long-lost-friend. He claimed to remember me and quickly explained that he was now working as an administrator at a business college.

When I expressed surprise at his career change, he launched into the story of his time at Meadows of Dan as though it had been bottled inside him for years. Now it all came bursting out.

"You know," he lamented. "I was trained to be an elementary school principal. That was what I had always wanted to do with my life. I assumed that I would always be an elementary school principal and I viewed that profession as my calling. I especially wanted to work with students in the Appalachian region. I liked the mountains and I admired the culture of the people there. I thought there I might be of some real service."

"I wasn't fired from the Meadows of Dan School, you

know," he assured me. "I just thought it was time to move on."

He went on to describe how he had accepted a job as principal at a new elementary school in North Carolina, just across the state line from Virginia. "It was my dream job. For years I had hoped to find such a position," he confessed.

"When I walked into that school on the morning of the first day of class, can you guess who was the first person I saw? There, swaggering down the hall, looking like he was ready to wrestle a buffalo – the very first student I encountered in my new school – was Duel."

Everyone is in awe of the lion tamer in a cage with half a dozen lions - everyone but a school bus driver.

— Anonymous

THE GAUNTLET

A cousin of mine, one who lives in a distant city, still gives me a call from time to time. Like me, he received all of his primary and secondary education at the Meadows of Dan School. He was just two years ahead of me, and as we advance further into our twilight years, we seem to spend more and more time talking about our old school days. Sometimes, our conversation will turn to the seventh grade and to Mrs. Fanny Anderson, the lady who taught that grade at Meadows of Dan for over forty years. We sometimes do imitations of Mrs. Anderson leading the seventh grade class in singing some of her favorite songs.

D'ye ken John Peel, with his coat so gay,
He lived at Beckwith, once on a day,
But now he has gone, faar awaaaaay, far away.
We shall ne'er hear his horn in the morning.

When I ask some other of my former schoolmates what they remember most about the seventh grade at Meadows of Dan School, they will usually recall how tough it was under the strict discipline maintained by Mrs. Anderson and how much homework she would pile on us. But another common recollection is about the songs we would sing, almost every morning, before our classes started for the day. Every song we sang in that class was from the "The New Blue Book of Favorite Songs," and Mrs. Anderson's favorites apparently were John

Peel, The Bonnets of Bonny Dundee, and The Battle Hymn of the Republic. We sang those songs many, many mornings in our seventh grade school year, and I recall us singing them with great gusto.

When we were singing about Bonny Dundee and John Peel, I think it unlikely that any of us were aware that either John Peel or the Laird of Claverhouse were actual historical figures. We, as mostly descendants of Scots-Irish and English immigrants, were unknowingly paying homage to our own history through those songs. I still wonder, as Mrs. Anderson led us in these songs with such enthusiasm, did she have an educational motive? She probably just liked them.

From almost the first day any of us started school at Meadows of Dan, we began hearing about how tough it was going to be when we got to the seventh grade. For every year thereafter, until we finally reached that grade, we would be told about the comeuppance we were going to face upon our arrival. Frustrated parents would often warn their errant children with predictions such as, "Just you wait 'til you get into the seventh grade. Mrs. Anderson will straighten you out in a hurry."

Even before I started to school, I had heard Coy Lee Yeatts tell about the time Mrs. Anderson came up from the back of the room and knocked Gene Barnard out of his desk with a geography book swung in one direction, and then knocked him out of his desk on the backswing. He claimed to have had no idea what he and Gene might have done wrong. When I asked my mom, who also taught at the Meadows of Dan School, if things like that really happened, she confirmed that they did.

She then tried to reassure me by telling me that all of that occurred years ago, when Mrs. Anderson was teaching in the old
school building and that she had mellowed considerably since
then. I continued to hear the stories and I was not reassured.

It was a given that we were going to get shaped up when
we got into the seventh grade. We thought it might be something like the military boot camp our fathers and older brothers
would tell us about. Then, as we got into the second and then
the third grades, we began to hear that the sixth grade, with Mrs.
Elizabeth Cock as the teacher, was not going to be a walk in the
park either.

At some point, we all heard the story about Miz Elizabeth walking into Mrs. Anderson's room one Friday afternoon
and announcing, "Lordy, I'm so tired. I just finished whuppin'
twenty-six kids." She then described to Mrs. Anderson her policy of recording each student's demerits for the week, and at the
end of it, all who had accumulated five or more got a paddling,
one lick for every demerit above four. Perhaps that was just an
especially bad week.

This policy probably seemed too complicated to Mrs.
Anderson. Whatever the offense, she didn't wait around. The
whack(s) it merited were delivered with the yardstick she kept
so readily at hand, forthwith, like a bolt from the blue.

When I first heard the "whuppin" story about Mrs.
Cock, it sounded really scary, but later I became hopeful. I ra-
tionalized that, if Mrs. Anderson was mellowing with the years,
maybe Miz Elizabeth was, too. Maybe she was really not going
to be all that strict. "I'll bet she was just trying to impress Mrs.

Anderson," I thought. "She was letting Mrs. Anderson know that she was not the only tough cookie teaching in that school." We were to learn just a few years later that Mrs. Cock's reputation was not simply a myth.

As our class proceeded, year by year, through the Meadows of Dan School, we were accompanied by the cloud of dread caused by the awareness that we were drawing ever nearer to the seventh grade. Miz. Elizabeth's sixth grade looming even nearer, was viewed with almost equal fear and trepidation. To us, the sixth and seventh grades were to be a rite-of-passage, a trial-by-fire which we must all endure to prove ourselves worthy of admission into the relative freedom of high school. Oh, how we were going to enjoy the eighth grade!

Back in the fourth grade, when life was still pretty good, Mrs. Pauline Cock, coincidentally a sister-in-law to Miz Elizabeth, was just about everyone's favorite teacher. She was patient and fair, and her students could tell that she genuinely wanted them to do well. But even Miz Polly, as we called her behind her back, could not be successful with all of the students all of the time.

One day her frustration boiled over as she was trying to help a student with some math problems. I was eavesdropping on their conversation, and it sounded as though the student she was trying to help, a boy who was quite a bit older than most of us in the class, expressed his preference to just be left alone .

Then I heard Miz Polly tell him, "Now Leonard, I know you can do these problems if you will just make an effort. Won't you even try? Don't you even want to pass math?"

"Oh, Miz Cock," he responded, with total respect. "I can do them math problems all right. Sometimes I solve a few of 'em on my own, just to prove to myself that I can. I kind of like doin' math problems, but I really don't want to pass math or nothin' else. I just want to get to be sixteen and get out of here. I aim to leave this school before I get to the seventh grade and have to take Miz Anderson. After I quit school, I'll get me a job and make some money."

I think, like the rest of us, he had heard that Mrs. Anderson whacked students who failed to do their math homework with a yard stick. It was rumored that Mrs. Anderson would go through a dozen or more heavy-duty yardsticks in a year. Oddly, the student talking to Miz Polly about quitting school was a big, tough kid that little squirts like me thought would have no reason to be scared of anything.

Needless to say, the young man was able to realize his ambition to not make it to the seventh grade without too much difficulty. He just bided his time, didn't cause much trouble, and skipped precisely as much school as he possibly could without getting his folks into trouble because of his truancy I don't think he was ever within the walls of the school from his sixteenth birthday on. The saddest part of the story is that he did not realize that he had already run a large part of the gauntlet by the time he dropped out, sometime near the end of the sixth grade.

By the fourth grade, we were pretty well resigned to the two-year gauntlet through which we would have to pass in the sixth and seventh grades. But then came the unexpected surprise; a fifth grade addition to the trial of endurance. We, or at least I, did not know that Mrs. Lucy Bowman was going to be so hard on us. From the day I entered the fifth grade, it was clear to me that it would now be at least three years before I could really begin enjoying school again. We all knew that we were going to catch the dickens when we got to the seventh grade; that was understood as inevitable, and we were even reconciled to what we were going to have to face in the sixth. But my experience with Miz Lucy in the fifth grade was totally unanticipated.

Miz Lucy was not an experienced teacher or even a trained educator, but someone who had been hired to teach on an emergency certificate instead. People sometimes make fun of the education classes that would-be teachers have to take as part of their training, and it is true that some of them are pretty simple. But I have observed, both as a student and as a teacher, there can be significant differences between the effectiveness of teachers who have been through an accredited teacher training program and those who have not. A lot of the folks in the community, however, held fast to the belief that "a hard teacher is a good teacher." For some of them, "hard" did not necessarily mean high academic standards, but the term "hard teacher" just meant one who would whack the dickens out of any student who caused them trouble.

There certainly was a shortage of trained teachers in Patrick County in the 40's and 50's, and sometimes the schools had to hire people who were less than adequately trained. Teachers were often considered successful if they could just make the students sit at their desks and behave themselves most of the time. There is no question that the teacher needs to be in control of the classroom, but there is a lot more to good teaching than that. Keeping an orderly classroom sometimes carried more weight than whether or not the kids learned their grammar and their math. That philosophy, I believe, explains why Miz Lucy was hired to be our fifth grade teacher.

My personal view of Miz Lucy is that she simply did not like her students very much. Or more precisely, she really disliked noisy little boys a lot. Fifth grade girls are typically a lot more mature than fifth grade boys, and some of the girls in our grade were mature enough and smart enough to behave like little ladies and really schmooze up to their teacher. This teacher seemed to think that the schmoozers were OK. Although it was pretty clear just what one needed to do to get along in the fifth grade, some of us boys were still just immature, silly, little kids.

One of my good friends in the fifth grade was Buddy Cockram. At the time I thought that he was the funniest human who had ever dwelt on earth. He, in return, appeared to appreciate my own efforts at elementary school humor. Since just about anything goofy that one of us did would send the other into convulsions of laughter, we were assigned desks opposite sides of the room for the entire year. That may have helped some, but when the teacher's back was turned, we could still make gestures and pantomimes that would send the other into hysterics. Unfortunately, when laughter erupted in Miz Lucy's class, it had serious consequences. Miz Lucy would call us jack o' lanterns while she was whomping us, because of the big grins we would have on our faces (before the whomping).

One of our fifth grade classes was called, *Health*, and Miz Lucy's approach to teaching it was to have the students take turns reading the text book out loud to the rest of the class. She didn't select the readers at random, but carefully scoped the class, calling upon anyone whose attention appeared to have wandered, even for a moment. And woe be it unto one, whom, if called upon to read, did not have the place where the last reader had stopped.

There was a list of vocabulary words at the end of each chapter in our health text, and much of the testing came from that list of words. Sometimes Miz Lucy would read the words out to us and we would have to spell the words and sometimes write down their definitions. About half of our grade in that class came from spelling the vocabulary words. We were supposed to learn how to spell words such as hydrochloric acid and pancreas and appendicitis. I suppose there was some benefit to all that emphasis on spelling somewhere down the road, but I was a really poor speller and the spelling requirement made my grade in that health class pretty dismal. I did leave the class able to spell pancreas, even though I still didn't know a pancreas from a porcupine.

I really don't think all this memorizing hurt me a lot. Most of us survived and moved on up to the sixth grade, on to level two of the three stage ordeal. It is only fair to reveal that some of my schoolmates remember Miz Lucy much more fondly than I do, probably because they were better behaved.

We had learned one thing about Mrs. Elizabeth Cock in advance, from just walking past the sixth grade class room; she was really fond of potted plants. When the door to her room was open, anyone could see that the window ledge was completely lined with green, shiny and healthy potted plants. There were begonias and gloxinias and even a philodendron that grew the whole length of one window ledge. It was obvious that they were very well cared for, and we were told that she would allow only a chosen few to assist with their care and feeding.

In the spring of the year that I was in the fourth grade, a rumor began to circulate around the school that something odd was happening to Miz Elizabeth's potted plants. Apparently, some strange vegetation was sprouting up amongst the begonias and gloxinias. This alien vegetation grew tall and it grew fast, and as it grew higher and higher it began to take on the appearance of…, well, it looked like…, yes, it definitely was. There were stalks of corn growing in among Miz Elizabeth's potted plants, and maybe some buckwheat too. How, even in a classroom in which about twenty five of the thirty-two students lived on farms that grew corn, could such a thing possibly happen? Perhaps some of the boys had just happened to come to class with some seed corn left in their pockets one day, and some of it accidentally fell into the flower pots. Probably they meant to drop it into the trash can.

When Miz Elizabeth realized that corn stalks were growing up through her flowers, she was furious.

"All right class, no one will get to go out for recess until the person who planted the corn in my flowers owns up to it."

Carlton Rakes really didn't know who the culprit was, but he just blurted out on a hunch, "That looks to me like something Fred Yeatts would do."

Miz Elizabeth knew her students pretty well:

"Freddie, did you plant corn in my flower pots?'

"Yes, Ma'am."

"Jimmie, did you help Freddie plant the corn?"

"Yes, Ma'am."

You might assume that, with Freddie and Jimmie being so truthful and everything, that she would have come up with a mild form of punishment such as making them wash the black-boards for a week. No, the lady was furious over this benign little prank, and in her own words, she popped their jaws real good.

Maybe the sixth grade wasn't all bad, taken in perspective. I learned to keep my head down and my mouth shut a bit more that year, a skill that helped me out in the next one. I don't remember Miz Elizabeth being too mean, at least for the folks who got their long division homework problems all done (a group which often did not include me). We also learned to multiply and divide fractions that year. When we were learning to divide fractions, Miz Elizabeth would not allow us to use the technique of inverting and multiplying, the way it was taught in our math book. She told us that students were not allowed to do that until they got into the seventh grade. Well, at least that gave us something to look forward to.

A year later we were entering into the *dreaded seventh grade*. Lots of plane geometry (my best subject), lots of geography (my favorite subject) and lots of English (never mind). We had been in two years of training for the seventh grade; we did our homework, we didn't talk out of turn, and we came in from recess on time. In other words, Mrs. Anderson's formidable reputation worked its magic on her students without her having to lift a finger.

Mrs. Anderson frequently left the room, apparently with full confidence that she had instilled enough discipline into her students that they would continue with their work, even in her absence. Such was not always the case, however. Fortunately, Mrs. Anderson always wore these very high-heeled shoes, and we could hear her click-clacking back down the hall in plenty of time to abandon whatever mischief we were engaged in and get back on task.

It was a pretty good year as I recall. We learned quite a bit, and I don't think I got whacked more than about a dozen times, much better than the previous two years. More than the corporal punishment occasionally delivered by our teacher, I remember fearing her stinging sarcasm. In her many years of experience, Mrs. Anderson had learned that words could hurt more than a yard stick. When we finally reached the end of the seventh grade, most of us felt that we had truly run the gauntlet and survived. Everyone worked really hard to pass, because nobody wanted to do that again.

Several years after graduating from Meadows of Dan High School, I attended a school reunion, after which a few of us gathered out at the top of the mountain for another reunion, of sorts, this one at the Lover's Leap Tavern. As we reminisced over a few beers, the subject turned to our teachers and to the terrors of the seventh grade, both real and imagined. As long as we were in a tavern and talking about the seventh grade, I thought it might be a good time to revisit some of the songs we used to sing in the mornings before class. "Anybody remember this?" I asked, and I just started singing…

>*To the Lords of convention, 'twas Claverhouse spoke.*
>*"E're the Kings crown go down, there are crowns to be broke.*

By half-way through the first stanza, a few others had joined in.

>*"So let each cavalier who loves honor and me,*
>*Let him follow the Bonnets of Bonny Dundee."*

The tavern was nearly full of Meadows of Dan school alumni that night, all of whom had Mrs. Fanny Anderson as their seventh grade teacher. Not everyone remembered the verses, but everyone joined in loudly on the chorus, literally rocking the tavern. The singing, I think, was not so much of a tribute to her as an unspoken recognition that not all of our seventh grade experience was bad.

>*Come fill up my cup, come fill up my can,*
>*Come saddle your horses and call out your men.*
>*Unhook the west port and let us go freeeeeee,*
>*For it's up to the Bonnets O' Bonny Dundee.*

The Other

In the decade following World War II, there was a serious shortage of teachers just about everywhere in the country. During the war, women had entered the workforce in large numbers, and some of these new job opportunities for women continued after the war had ended. Women now had career options other than nursing, teaching, or housewifery. The number of men going into teaching was reduced for several years following the war, simply because there were fewer men available to train as teachers during the war years.

The teacher shortage was particularly acute for small rural school systems such as the one in Patrick County, Virginia. Some of the smaller schools within the system, such as the one at Meadows of Dan, had an especially difficult time attracting teachers. How many newly-minted education professionals would want to begin their careers in a rural community where they would have no social life and little opportunity for economic advancement? Unless one had family there, or was just attracted to a quiet rural life style, why would he or she take a job there? Especially in a high school where the teaching load could be five or six different subjects, plus a study-hall and possibly even coaching one or two sports.

There was a story about the teacher shortage that was making the rounds in Patrick County back then. According to the tale, as the end of the summer and the beginning of the school year approached, and the county would never have all of its teaching positions filled. The school superintendent would then go and stand on a busy corner in a nearby town such as Roanoke or Winston Salem. There, like a military recruiter, he would stop likely looking prospects and ask them the question, "You wouldn't by chance be interested in teaching in Patrick County this fall, would you?" I don't believe the story is true, but it would account for some of the wild characters who would show up from time to time and teach a year or two at county schools such as Meadows of Dan.

The integrity of many small, rural schools such as the one at Meadows of Dan was maintained during the years of teacher shortages by the core of hard-working, dedicated teachers who highly valued their community and their school. I was taught by several such teachers during my years at that institution, and to those dedicated professionals, I will remain forever grateful. There are too many to list them all, but I am especially appreciative of Ms. Ruth Jean Bolt, who conveyed to us an appreciation of art and music while also teaching us that our mountain heritage was something of which we should be proud. I am grateful to teachers such as Mrs. Eloise Shelor, from whom I learned to write a correct sentence. And, although I did a lot of complaining at the time, Mrs. Frances Underwood, who gave us tons of algebra homework, was one math teacher who actually graded it all!

I could go on and on about how important some of these dedicated educators have been in my life, but I also cannot help but recall some others. There were a number of folk hired to fill in during the teacher shortages, who from all indications, should have been in some other line of work. Most of them came and went in a short period of time, but the memory of some lingered long after they were gone.

Who could (or should) forget a general science teacher who told the class that men have one less rib than women and that thunder is caused by clouds bumping together? But when I mention the temporary home economics teacher who planned a lunchroom meal of baked yams, boiled Irish potatoes, and rice, I should also mention that the supplies for our school lunches in those days sometimes ran short.

In the 1950's, the main focus of Patrick County High Schools was Vocational Agriculture for the boys and Home Economics for the girls. Patrick County Schools did a credible job in educating the students in these fields I imagine, but unfortunately, the nation was on the cusp of drastic economic and industrial change at just that time. Who could know that the small family farm was going to almost disappear in just a few years, and that more and more women would be seeking careers outside of the home? Nerdy subjects such as mathematics or chemistry definitely were not a high priority at Meadows of Dan or any other Patrick County high school that I was aware of. That is probably just as well, because the demand for those courses was really not there, and it would have been very difficult to find the people to teach them anyway.

Whenever I wonder where some of these transient teachers were found, my thoughts always turn to Mr. Wallace Berensky (not his real name). Whenever there is a shortage of teachers, it is usually the science and math instruction that suffers most. Mr. Berenski was hired to teach science, among other courses, with his main credential being that he was an ordained minister in a denomination which was never revealed. A few of the parents may have been pleased that he was hired, however, since they could be confident that their kids were not going to be indoctrinated in any modern scientific theories such as evolution.

In the fall one year, there were five or six of us who had expressed a strong interest in taking chemistry. Mr. Prillaman, the principal, was sympathetic, but unfortunately there was simply no one available who was qualified to teach chemistry. They had just hired Mr. Berensky, however, and since he was teaching only four other courses, he generously agreed to teach the chemistry class. Immediately, the problems began, not all of which were of Mr. Berensky's own making. He was from Pennsylvania, you see, from "someplace up north" in the local jargon. Some folks from our neck of the woods were just naturally suspicious of him, and he of them.

Most of us at the Meadows of Dan School barely knew that there ever was such an organization as the Ku Klux Klan, and certainly none of us had ever known anyone who was a member. But when Mr. Berensky foolishly expressed his concern that the Klan might be active in the area, someone began feeding his paranoia by slipping little charred wooden crosses onto his desk and under the windshield wipers of his car. When he reported the incidents to local law enforcement, the investigating deputy pointed out that, since the charred crosses appeared to be made from popsicle sticks, hard-core clansmen were probably not the ones responsible.

If the man had just admitted that the chemistry course was outside of his field of knowledge and made a deal with the school's science nerds, I think that together we could have labored through the text and possibly learned a fair amount. We were semi-serious students, after all, and when we mostly self-taught our physics class, the result was a somewhat other than total disaster.

But Mr. B took an entirely different approach to the course, attempting to bluff his way through material that he clearly did not understand and for which he had inadequate time to prepare. But the real disaster began when he decided to allow the chemistry students to do some unsupervised lab experiments. Within a single week, we had exhausted (pun intended) virtually every known method of producing hydrogen sulfide gas and had begun branching out into the production of explosives. Our chemistry teacher decided that the solution to that problem was to purge the lab of all dangerous chemicals, but unfortunately, he had no idea which ones they were.

The teacher had become alarmed a few days earlier when someone created a small hydrogen explosion by dropping a little dab of sodium metal into a beaker of water. So when the time came to dispose of the "dangerous" chemicals, the large jar containing blocks of sodium metal submerged in kerosene was at the top of his list. His solution? Why, wash it down the sink, of course. We honestly tried to stop him, warning him that the sodium metal might explode, even inside the drain and under water, but he thought we just were putting him on.

When it became clear that he really was going to try to

wash the stuff down the sink, we scattered. A couple of students ran out into the hall while the rest of us ran to the other end of the classroom and took shelter behind the desks. Mr. Berensky was chiding us for clowning around in chemistry class as he inverted the jar over the sink and turned on the water.

Immediately, the sodium began hissing and gurgling. Then, a small flame erupted, fortunately warning Mr. B and giving him enough time to take a few steps away from the sink and toward the door just before the main event. I was peeping over the top of a desk when the loud boom occurred and our esteemed instructor went sailing out through the open door.

The massive old slate sink which confined the explosion probably saved us all. There were no injuries, other than temporary hearing impairment for most present, and the only damage to the building was the ruptured sink and drain, plus a dozen or so of the panes blown out of the room's windows. .

Wally Berensky's reaction? He rushed to tell the principal that he had tried to prevent the students from dumping the sodium down the sink, but that we had done the deed counter to his explicit instructions. The class was outraged. Before the chemistry class explosion, we thought of Mr. Berenski merely as an incompetent, but basically harmless, buffoon. Now we saw him as a duplicitous liar. Our principal, fortunately, knew the score and believed us students instead of the instructor. But since we were only a couple of weeks into the course, and because it affected such a small number of students, the Principal talked everyone in the chemistry class into a math class taught by a different teacher. The math class was not that great, since was taught by someone whose specialty was history, but it was definitely much safer.

Although I recall Mr. Berensky's dishonesty to this day, the penalty for not having taken high school chemistry was far less than I had feared. When I took chemistry in college, I observed that that there was almost no correlation between students having had chemistry in high school and doing well in in college chemistry. From listening to some stories of other's experiences, I concluded that many high school chemistry courses were disasters, if not in the exactly the same way as ours.

I spent my senior year in Meadows of Dan High school thinking that my future was doomed. Unlike some of my cousins who attended large city schools, I had not been able to take chemistry or trigonometry. It really mattered much less than I feared.

There was at least one class available at Meadows of Dan High School which I have long regretted not taking. If I had taken Typing, it would have been a great help to me in school and at work. But back in the nineteen-fifties, forty years before personal computers, I thought only people who were going to be secretaries needed to know how to type.

We've arranged a civilization in which most crucial elements profoundly depend on science and technology. We have also arranged things so that almost no one understands that science and technology. This is a prescription for disaster. We might get away with it for a while, but sooner or later this combustible mixture of ignorance and power is going to blow up in our faces.

— Carl Sagan

Take Good Care of your Tools
(and Your Tools Will Take Care of You)

Students are typically not very good judges of the quality of the education they are receiving while they are still in the process. They certainly can tell whether they enjoy the class, and that is important; they can also tell if the teacher or the students are in control of the agenda, and that is even more important. But the true test of the value of a course one takes in school often comes later, sometimes much later.

My wife, obviously irritated, stamped into the room holding up a screwdriver which appeared to have endured a long and useful life. "Is this the best screwdriver we have?" she demanded to know.

She was frustrated because she was unable to tighten up some electrical connections on her kiln. The blade of the battered old screwdriver kept slipping out of the slots in the screw heads. I looked at the screwdriver she was holding and then went searching in my tool box. I found a larger one and a smaller one, but the only Goldilocks screwdriver we could find was the one she had just been trying to use. It must have been worn because it was just the right size for so many uses. I handed her the larger screwdriver I had found and returned to my work.

In a moment she was back, exasperated. "The blade on this screwdriver is too thick. It won't even go into the slot on the screws," she complained. She is an independent soul and likes to fix things for herself when she can. I know by now that if she says something won't work, it really won't work.

Just the same, I am sure that I must have heaved a loud sigh of weariness, reluctantly leaving my work again to go out into the garage to have another look at the problem. First, I tried the larger screwdriver, which, just like she said, had a blade too thick to go into the screw slot. And when I tried the smaller one, it slipped right out of the slot. Then I took another look at the blade of the screwdriver which started it all.

"This screwdriver is about worn-out. It needs to be sharpened," I announced to my wife.

She looked at me as if I had lost my mind. "You're kidding. Who ever heard of sharpening a screwdriver?"

"I am not kidding. When old flat blade screwdrivers get worn off on the corners like this one…" I presented the screwdriver to her for close examination, "you can't keep them in the screw slot. But they can be made to work a lot better by sharpening them. You just have to know how."

Sweetie looked at the badly worn screwdriver with a skeptical gaze before I carried it over to the bench grinder. There, I ground about one-eighth of an inch off the end of the blade, sharpened the end back to its original thickness, smoothed the taper on the flat of the blade, and ground the burrs off the sides. The whole process took about five minutes.

"Here. Try this." I presented the newly rejuvenated screwdriver to her.

"Hey, it works just great!" she called out a minute later. I don't want to brag, but this sort of thing is the main reason she keeps me around.

At dinner that night the subject of the screwdrivers

came up again. Although her step-father had been very much of a handyman, she had never heard of him, or anyone else for that matter, sharpening a screwdriver.

"I had never heard of such a thing. Where did you learn how to sharpen a screwdriver?" she asked.

I had to think for only a moment. "Why from Nelson Thomas, I am sure. Mr. Thomas was the vocational agriculture teacher at Meadows of Dan High School."

My wife thought that was very strange. "Vocational agriculture? I didn't know you took vocational agriculture courses in high school."

"Actually, I didn't," I responded, straining to recall events from most of a lifetime ago. "But when we were in the eighth grade, we had to choose from a selection of short elective courses. We had to choose short courses from shop, home economics, music appreciation, art, typing, a lot of different stuff. One of the short courses I took was shop. It was only eight or nine weeks long, but one of the things I remember from that course was Mr. Thomas teaching us how to sharpen a screwdriver."

"Did you learn anything else in that class? Eight weeks is not a very long time."

"Oh, I think I learned a lot of useful stuff in that class, maybe more than in most of my classes. I do remember that we had to learn the correct names of all of the hand tools. Naming the tools was mostly what was asked on the final exam. One thing I remember that we would call the scratch awl a screech owl, just for fun."

Later, I began thinking more about the short introductory shop class I had taken over fifty years ago. It was amazing how much I could remember learning in that class, and how much of it I had used over the years without even realizing it. One useful thing that Mr. Thomas strongly emphasized was how important it is to properly care for and organize one's tools. One of his favorite quotes was obviously directed at students who would be future farmers and craftsmen.

"Take good care of your tools," he told us, "so they can take care of you." Even today, I think that is good advice.

I can recall so clearly Mr. Thomas's description of how, when he was a young child in the midst of the Great Depression, the collection of tools in his father's tool box consisted of one worn-out flat-blade screwdriver, one equally worn pair of slip-joint pliers, and a claw hammer with friction tape on the handle and the peen worn flat. I remembered wondering at the time if that was what prompted him to become a vocational agriculture/shop teacher. That way, he would have access to all of the good tools anyone would ever need. I also recall thinking that the tool box he described sounded a whole lot like the one at our house. As I looked around, several of the other kids in the class were smiling knowingly. Apparently, about three basic tools in the tool box at home was the norm for that class.

I remembered that Mr. Toms, as the students often called him, followed his description of his family's tool box with the admonition, "if you want to tear stuff up, if you want to round off nuts and gouge out screw slots so that you can never get something fixed, just use slip-joint pliers on the nuts and the wrong-size screw driver in the screws. He then went on to give us a short list of basic tools he recommended that everyone should have for making small repairs around the home and farm. But never use pliers on a nut, he repeated. To this day, it has to be a desperate situation for me to use pliers to try to loosen a nut. But that is true only if vice-grips don't count.

About the same time we learned that screw drivers can be rejuvenated by sharpening them, we also learned that hammers wear out. I did not even know what the word peen meant before Mr. Thomas described and showed us that even claw hammers have a slight *peen* or curvature on the face of their hammering surface. If the curvature on the face becomes worn flat through use or gets badly roughened, it becomes much harder to drive a nail without bending it. This is not a repairable problem, and Mr. Thomas spent a considerable amount of time explaining how one should never abuse his hammer (snicker, snicker) or it will need to be replaced.

Mr. Thomas also told us about how, when he was a young boy, he would sometimes be allowed to ride one of their horses out on the road on Sunday afternoons. He described how, although these were draft horses, if he came upon an audience such as a family sitting out on their front porch, he would whip the horse into a gallop and go by the house as fast as it could run. He would see the folks looking at him, talking to each other and nodding knowingly as he rode by. He said he assumed at the time that the folks were commenting on his riding, saying things such as, "That boy sure can ride, can't he?" Mr. Thomas said that he later learned they were really saying, "Just look at that dummy. He's going to ruin a good horse and maybe break his fool neck in the bargain."

At the time I wondered why he was telling such a tale, one which surely had no relevance in the age of the automobile. Later it occurred to me that if one substituted "car" for "horse" and "drive" for "ride," it applied to us teenagers. He was teaching us with a timely parable.

After the first few lectures, we migrated from the classroom out into the big shop for demonstrations in the use of the woodworking power tools. Mr. Toms began by making us all put on safety glasses before demonstrating how to use a bench grinder to sharpen a screwdriver. After the demonstration he told us that if we would bring in our worn screwdrivers from home, we would be allowed to sharpen them in the shop. Several of us took him up on the offer and we showed up at the next class with a collection of some really pitiful looking screw drivers. Imagine our disappointment when he made us clamp the screwdrivers in a vise and then sharpen them with a flat file instead of getting to use a bench grinder! We were not even allowed to use a power tool as basic as a bench grinder! But there were compensations.

Mr. Thomas made the mistake of telling us that the tools we were using to sharpen our screwdrivers were called "bastard files." We then had ourselves a great old time using the forbidden word within the pretext of normal conversation.

"Are you through with that flat bastard yet?"

"Not quite. Couldn't you use a half-round sum-bitch?"

It was made clear from the beginning that we novice

shop students were not going to be allowed to use the big power tools. In a single class period, however, Mr. Thomas demonstrated the basics of the use of most of them. The major concern in each case was how to use the tool safely, with eye protection emphasized first and foremost. As we watched the demonstrations, the vision of every one near the machine was protected by a pair of ancient and poorly fitting safety glasses. The lenses were so abraded and pitted that many of the significant details of the demonstration could not be seen.

As we gathered around the big table saw, Mr. Thomas first demonstrated how to adjust the position of the fence and the height of the circular saw blade, then he showed us where one should stand while sawing. Then he explained how one should use a push stick when cutting small pieces to keep from getting your hand too close to the blade. In the process of the demonstration, he ripped a wide board into two narrower ones and then ripped one of the narrow boards into slender sticks.

When we were directed over to the big wood lathe, it had a piece of wood that looked like the beginnings of a baseball bat already mounted in it. As we watched from a respectful distance, Mr. Thomas revved up the lathe and cut a few shavings from the object, then shut it down and reminded us that this was the closest we peons would ever be allowed to approach such a powerful and dangerous tools. That was, unless we opted to sign up for some vocational agriculture courses in the future. Then, near the end of the introduction to large power tools, Mr. Thomas gave us a demonstration which neither I nor any other student who was there that day shall ever forget.

Mr. Nelson Thomas was a very intelligent man who also happened to be rather ungraceful and somewhat accident prone. That day, he strode purposefully over to the big seven inch, industrial-model wood joiner near the center of the shop, placed his hand on the joiner table, then turned and addressed the group: "Now boys," he declared, "this is the most dangerous machine we have in this shop. There are more eyes and fingers lost using the joiner than all other power tools combined." To emphasize the danger, he pivoted the guard away from its normal position over the blades so that we could clearly see the hazard.

Mr. Thomas then reached down under the joiner and pushed the green button on the control box, causing the machine to roar into life. "One big problem when using the joiner," he shouted, straining to make himself heard over the din of the powerful motor, "is that when the blades get dull, they tend to grab the piece you are feeding in and jerk it away from your hand. If you are holding onto the work piece and putting weight down on it, your hand can be pulled into the blades before it can be released."

Mr. Thomas had been holding a couple of pieces of wood in his hand as he spoke. Now he placed the larger piece of wood on top of the joiner table and butted it against the fence near the spinning blades.

"You should never feed a small work piece to the joiner with your hand, like this," he shouted, sliding the small board up to within an inch or two of the whirring blades. Turning back towards us students and holding up two smaller sticks, he proclaimed, "you should always feed the work into the blades with push blocks, like this."

Then, as he turned and leaned back over the joiner, something strange occurred. I was unable to see exactly what happened, but the work piece and the push block went sailing off of the end of the joiner table and across the shop floor. At the same instant, Mr. Thomas gave an agonizing "Aaaagh!" and grabbed his right hand with his left one. As he ran from the joiner towards the wash room, we could see that his left hand was clutching his badly bleeding right thumb, a small part of which appeared to be missing. At the door to the washroom, he turned back toward his class of gaping students.

"Elmer, shut down the joiner!" Mr. Thomas shouted back to an older student working in the shop. "Class dismissed." Then he disappeared into the washroom.

Nelson Thomas was surely a good sport about the unfortunate event, and he even turned his embarrassing accident into a teaching moment. In class the next day, with the thumb wrapped in an enormous white bandage, he held up his injured hand and waved it back and forth in front of the class.

"The lesson for today is…" and Mr. Thomas held his bandaged thumb up above his head, "that you should do as I say, not do as I do."

On our way out of the shop building at the end of that class, one student summed up the whole unfortunate event. "You know," he seriously commented. "Mr. Toms don't have a long enough thumb to do that demonstration many more times."

The nation which honors mediocrity in philosophy more than it honors excellence in plumbing will have excellence in neither its plumbing nor its philosophy. Neither its pipes nor its theories will hold water.

— Anonymous

Wisdom from the Mouths of Babes

These third graders could not really understand all that was being reported on the evening news, but they could understand enough that it frightened them. One reason they were scared was because the adults all seemed so worried. Even the announcers on television, the same talking heads who usually announced the day's events in such a calm, boring way, seemed to be grimly concerned.

One October evening, the regular television program had been interrupted by a news bulletin announcing that the United States was going to enforce a naval blockade of Cuba. This was an act that could lead to war with the Soviet Union, the announcer said. Three nights later, the regular programming was interrupted again, first the with news about what was by then being called the "Cuban missile crisis" followed by a speech by President Kennedy. Even these young school kids knew that for *The Andy Griffith Show* to be interrupted for a speech by the President of the United States, something really serious must be going on.

To everyone, the really frightening thing was the reason being given for the blockade. Our "spy plane" flights over Cuba had revealed that the Soviet Union had established missile bases in there. The television announcers explained that the missiles in Cuba were almost certainly armed with nuclear warheads and were surely aimed at American cities. Those nuclear armed missiles could reach everywhere in the lower part of the United States, they said, as they kept referring to the fact that

Cuba was only ninety miles away.

Nikita Khrushchev, the premier of the Soviet Union, was threatening to retaliate against the blockade, declaring it to be an act of war and implying that the missiles might be used. With Soviet nuclear missiles bases now located in Cuba, it seemed that a nuclear war very soon was a real possibility. These third graders may not have had much of a concept of the term "naval blockade," but they had basic conceptions of what a "nuclear missile" was and what "nuclear war" could mean. For most of their lives they had been told that Russia was the enemy, a communist country which was bent on destroying the United States. Now, they were being told, this just might be the time the Russians were going to try to do it.

Most of these third graders were barely aware that there was a state named Florida, but they were unaware of its 450 mile length, not including the additional 125 miles of the Florida Key archipelago. The ninety mile distance that the broadcasters kept referring to is the distance from the northern coast of Cuba to the southernmost one of the Florida Keys, Key West. This was the first time many of these children had ever heard of Cuba, and the fact that it is about a thousand miles from Meadows of Dan could have been some consolation to them, had they been aware of it. Most of what had registered with the youngsters, when they listened to the newscasts, however, was that the Russians, along with their nuclear missiles, were in Cuba, just ninety miles away. This was a scary notion to just about everyone in the country. The fact that the government had generously provided all of the nation's elementary schools with civil defense films describing how school children should duck under their desks and cover their heads if the room was illuminated by the flash of an atomic explosion did not make them feel any more secure.

The third grade students began asking their teacher, Mrs. Eunice, some really serious questions as soon as the first bell rang on that October morning in 1962. "Was there going to be a war? Were the Russians going to drop atomic bombs on the United States? How close by might some of the bombs land? Could the Russians really hit the country with missiles anywhere they wanted? Would we launch missiles back at the Russians? Should we launch missiles at the Russians first? What would the world be like afterward, if the countries fired their nuclear missiles at each other?"

Eventually, the questions got down to the really scary details. "If there was a war using atomic missiles, would everyone in the world be killed? Would everyone be killed right away, or would a lot of the people get sick and die later, just like they were telling us on the news? Was there any place in the world that would be safe?"

The teacher was certainly no expert on nuclear weapons or civil defense, but she could not simply dismiss these students' concerns. She was very worried herself, and she thought that she would be doing the students no favor by simply assuring them that nothing bad was going to happen and that everything was going to be okay. She too had been watching the news. Her best response, she decided, would be to try and answer the students' questions as completely and honestly as she could.

Maybe they would feel better after they had given voice to their worst fears.

"Yes, the United States and the Soviet Union were making threats to each other that sounded as though we could possibly go to war."

"Yes, if there was a war, it might be one in which atomic weapons would be used. And if the war started, it could happen that both of the two countries would attack each other's cities with atomic bombs."

"Why do the Russians hate us? Well, I really don't think that the Russian people hate the American people, and I don't think that we hate them. Often, the leaders of one country find that it is easier to control their own people if they can make them think that the people of other countries are their enemies and are a danger to them. The Leaders of Nations have been doing that sort of thing for as far back as we have any history to tell us about it."

"No, there was no reason to think that Russia would bomb Meadows of Dan. And they would have no reason to bomb Stuart, or even Martinsville, for that matter."

"No, that did not necessarily mean that we would be completely safe here in the mountains. When atomic bombs explode, they stir up dust and other stuff which has been made radioactive. When something is radioactive, it gives off invisible rays that can harm you. You might think of it as being a poison, but it is a kind of poison that does not have to be eaten and it can harm you even through walls and through clothing. The radioactive material produced by the bombs is sucked high up into the air and can travel long distances before it drifts back down to the ground. That material can make people sick for a long time after a bomb has been exploded. That is what the newscasters mean when they talk about fallout. It would probably be many years before people could return to a town where an atomic bomb has been exploded, and the same might be true for some places many miles away.

"Yes, atomic bombs have been dropped on cities before. The United States dropped two of them on Japan in World War II. Many, many thousands of people died. Yes, the atomic bombs and missiles that America and Russia are threatening each other with now are much larger than the ones that were used then. And the United States and the Soviet Union each have many such bombs, maybe thousands."

"Yes, I think that a war with atomic bombs and missiles is just about the most horrible thing that I can imagine. Yes, I do think we should pray that such an awful thing will never happen. So let's all bow our heads and each of us will pray very hard that we will never have another war."

After the prayers had been said and most of the children had given voice to the worst of their fears, they seemed to be somewhat calmed. Most appeared willing to go on with their normal school routine, but Janie was not quite ready. The tiny girl with stringy pigtails, sitting near the front of the room, appeared to be inconsolable. She sat rigidly in her desk, her lips trembling and tears streaming down her cheeks. Miz Eunice went over to Janie and took her by her hands, hoping to give the child some sense of security.

"Now Janie, I really do feel that things are going to be all right," she told her. "The men who run both of our countries are very smart, and I don't think either America or Russia wants war. I think that surely our leaders will figure out some way to make it all work out."

Janie looked up at her teacher through her tear-filled eyes and blurted out her deepest feelings. "Well, if there's gonna be a war, with 'tomic bombs fallin' everwhere and everthing like that, I'd ruther have the first'un what falls to hit me right top th' head."

I believe Janie spoke for us all that day.

Ours is a world of nuclear giants and ethical infants. We know more about war that we know about peace, more about killing than we know about living.

— Gen. Omar N. Bradley

A Soldier in the Cold War

My dad used to talk a lot about how tough things were back in the thirties, back when he was coming of age here in these mountains. He said that about the only two options the young folk had for making a living were farming or leaving, and neither of those worked very well in the depression years. He would then tell me about men he had known who spent many of the years of their youth, hitch hiking and hoboing, looking for some kind of job. He tried it himself, for a short time, and he did not recommend it.

All that changed during World War II. By the forties and fifties, there were some other possible ways of earning a living here. Textile mills and furniture factories had opened up in towns that were only twenty or thirty miles away, and the improved roads made it easy to get to the jobs there. That created a third option; staying here in these mountains and commuting to a factory job somewhere in a town. But I still wondered what else there might be out there.

As the months of my senior year of high school rolled by, I was dogged by worries about the future. My high school days were coming to an end and I had no idea what I wanted to do with my life. As I looked around at what the people I knew were doing to earn their daily bread, I really did not see a lot of appealing possibilities.

There was no such thing as a guidance counselor at our school and I was clueless about the potential careers that might exist. I knew just a few people who could serve as role models or help me learn more about what might be available. Both of my parents were born and had lived their entire lives in Meadows of Dan. My mom attended Radford College and had a long career of teaching elementary school. My dad had a seventh grade education, worked as a mechanic for the highway department, and tried to do a little farming on the side. Although neither parent ever told that they planned on my going to college, Mom did mention that it was something that perhaps I should consider.

Maybe I did have some mechanical ability inherited from my dad, but I didn't want to be a farmer/mechanic like him. It wasn't that I did not admire his skill in what he did. But I did hope to find a career which did not require the twelve hours of work he typically put in for six days every week. Other than hoping to someday earn enough to support a family, making money was not something I thought much about at that time.

While searching out role models who might help me plan my future, I talked with an older cousin who was studying to be an electrical engineer. He had been in school for what seemed like years and years. Today he would probably be called a science geek, and he was always wrapped up in whatever it was that he was doing. But he did take time to impress on me what a tough time he was having in his study of electrical engineering.

I also had some serious conversations with an uncle who was working as a journalist for a newspaper in Richmond, but he just mostly complained about the constant pressure placed on him by his job. Another uncle, one who worked for DuPont, had to change shifts every couple of weeks and never seemed to get caught up on his sleep.

I used to listen with fascination when a neighbor, Mr. Loy Harris, would tell about working on high steel construction jobs in New York during the depression. He told that he and his brothers were able to get jobs working on the Empire State Building because of their black hair and eyes. They were able to pass themselves off as Mohawk Indians, people who were known for their ability to perform high steel work. That kind of work paid well and sounded truly exciting, but Mr. Harris used to joke that a tow head like me couldn't do that kind of work.

The two or three men I knew who were teachers seemed to like their jobs But teaching at a small high school like Meadows of Dan would probably mean teaching five different subjects, coaching one or two sports teams, and making very little money. About the only attraction I could find in teaching was that it appeared to be a little easier than farming and had a retirement plan. Had I seriously wanted to be a farmer, it would have been a problem because my family did not own enough good land to provide a decent living. Dad used to say, only partially as a joke, that half of our farmland was a rocky hillside and the other half was a swamp.

Most of the options which appealed to me at all would require additional schooling, and I knew that my going to college would be a burden for my parents. Another option to consider, however, was going into military service. Thinking that I could go to college on the G.I. Bill after serving in the military,

I decided that "signing up" right after high school was a reasonable plan. But the original "Servicemen's Readjustment Act," usually referred to as *The G.I. Bill,* expired in 1956, and the congressional act that replaced it did not allow for "peacetime educational benefits." The full G.I. bill, which included educational benefits, would not be reinstated until the unpleasantness in Southeast Asia began ramping up in the 1960's.

My dad, who served in the Second World War, had made it clear to me more than once that he thought I could use some of the discipline one learns from being in the military. I think he was even more disappointed than I was when we learned that the educational benefits in the G.I. Bill had expired. Dad was also very patriotic, and he really promoted the idea to me that I should spend some time in service to my country. As I approached the end of my senior year of high school, however, Mom and Dad and both assured me, if college was what I really wanted, they would find a way to send me.

While my parents indicated that they would be pleased for me to continue my education, my grandmother offered the opinion that going to college would just be my way of avoiding hard work. She did, however, offer to help me further my education if I wanted to become a preacher.

I understood from the beginning that my folks were not offering to send me to just any old school to study whatever might strike my fancy. The assumptions were that I would take advantage of the reasonable tuition offered by a state institution and that I would major in something that would enable me to get a job. Then my dad revealed that for several years, he had been putting the milk checks into a savings account. That, he said, would be available to me, if and when I decided to go to college. The account contained enough money so that, by choosing carefully, I might be able to attend a state university for a couple of years.

Cost was not the only consideration that should affect my choice, I was told. Not only did my folks tell me that I must select a college which was affordable, but it should be one not too far from home. The school would also have to be one that would find my high school academic record acceptable (scratch the University of Virginia). These requirements quickly whittled the list of potential colleges down to three: Appalachian State Teachers College, the University of Tennessee, and Virginia Polytechnic Institute. These institutions all indicated that they would accept me as a student, but the best deal was to be found at Appalachian State Teachers College in Boone, North Carolina. Even though the tuition there was somewhat higher for students who were not residents of North Carolina, it was still the least expensive of the three. The registrar at ASTC told me that the Federal Government had low-interest loans available, a part of which would be forgiven for graduates who taught in public schools for a few years. The financial advantages plus the fact that it was little more than a hundred miles from home moved Appalachian to the top of my list.

A summer of hot and hard construction work helped remove any doubts I may have had about the value of a college education. The end of August found me enrolling at Appalachian State Teachers College, still with no idea of what I should select as a major. The easiest courses for me in high school were social studies, but if one is going to teach, I thought, it should be in a field that one really likes. And, it should be a major that could also be useful in another career, should one find that he does not like teaching. I followed my advisor's instructions and signed up for basic courses that I would have to take, no matter what my major, for that first term.

It was early on a Saturday morning in October of 1957 that my epiphany occurred. The clock radio switched on at precisely 7:00 a.m., and the sonorous voice of well-known radio commentator Paul Harvey filled the dormitory room. (One can tell by the unheard of hour for a college student to be waking up on a Saturday that I was fresh off the farm.)

My roommate jumped out of his bed and grumpily headed for the radio to switch it off, but what we heard from the commentator caused the roommate to freeze in his tracks and jolted me out of bed and to wide awake.

"Good morning Americans," he intoned. "We awake from our slumber this fine morning to find a strange new object sailing above through the heavens! As you listen to this radio broadcast, a man-made satellite is circling the Earth, orbiting at an altitude of some three hundred miles, just above our heads, in the scale of space! This celestial intruder makes its trip around the globe every ninety minutes, invading the skies above our nation some sixteen times a day!"

"But the man-made moon was not put into space by the nation which we believe to be the scientific leader of the world. This was not the technological triumph of the country that invented the electric light and the atom bomb, the great nation that freed the world from tyranny in two world wars. This first tin moon in space was placed in its orbit around the Earth by the scientists of the Union of Soviet Socialist Republics, Russia. Slaves, dragging their chains, have out-distanced free men, dragging their feet!"

According to the commentator, the leaders of the United States were in a panic! We had fallen behind the Soviet Union in the exploration of space! We were in danger of losing the cold war! The survival of the free world was at stake! The commies had placed a satellite called *Sputnik* in orbit about the globe, and it sped through space at 18,000 miles per hour, beeping at us, mocking us, each time it passed overhead!

Now we were all asking the question, what else could that satellite do? Would it interfere with our television reception or listen in on our telephones? Was it equipped with cameras or radio listening devices? Could it be carrying weapons that would be used as a constant threat, literally held over the heads of the free world below?

We now know that our scientists (or our spies) figured out most of the critical information about Sputnik in a matter of a few days, but it would be many years before the American Public learned that the only instrumentation carried by that first tin moon was the radio transmitter that beeped at us as it flew overhead. True, the Soviets had launched the first satellite into orbit around the earth, but its primary value was political, not scientific. Like most people, my vocabulary did not even contain the words *orbit* or *satellite* prior to October 1957.

Paul Harvey dedicated the remainder of his fifteen minute program to a harangue about the sorry state of American education. While he blamed the American educational system in general, he directed his most strident criticism at those he assumed to be responsible for the dismal lack of knowledge demonstrated by our nation's youth in the areas of mathematics, science, and technology. (Does that sound familiar?) As the radio newsman belabored the lack of American resolve which led to this critical failure, the decision which would affect the remainder of my life was being made for me!

Mathematics should be my major! Math was not very easy for me and it was not my favorite subject, but I liked it well enough that I was willing to work at it. I had made decent math grades in high school, and now my country needed me! The announcer made it sound as though becoming a mathematics teacher could be a career that would truly be of service to my country. Based on what he was saying, a mathematics teacher would surely have no trouble in finding a job, anywhere in the country one might want to live.

From the first moment of that broadcast, my destiny was clear. As a mathematics teacher, I could earn my daily bread while being of service to my country. I would be a soldier in the cold war.

"Perhaps the most valuable result of all education is the ability to make yourself do the things you have to do, whether you like it or not."

— Thomas Huxley

The Magic Carburetor

It sounded reasonable enough to me. Why would a lowly teenager who did not yet even have his driver's license, have any reason to doubt the tale? Why couldn't an obscure genius invent a carburetor which would quickly and easily convert the family car into a vehicle capable of traveling 200 miles on a single gallon of gasoline?

This was the 1950's and gasoline was selling for about a quarter a gallon. My brother-in-law, a certifiable car nut and graduate of Virginia Polytechnic Institute, was introducing me to "The Legend of the Magic Carburetor." It was a fascinating story of how his roommate at Tech had known this genius of a mechanical engineering major who had invented a new type of carburetor.

According to my brother in law, the roommate had reliable information that the genius had bolted his newly invented carburetor onto a 1954 model Oldsmobile 88. He then proceeded to drive that powerful and thirsty car all the way from Virginia to Southern California on a single tank of gas. That would have been an average fuel mileage of almost 200 miles per gallon. Those who believed the story talked a lot about the 200 MPG carburetor.

As the story went, the genius soon dropped out of school to create a company to manufacture these carburetors and quickly became a very wealthy man. It was claimed that he became rich however, not from building and selling carburetors, but from the millions that Standard Oil Company supposedly paid him for the only existing model of his carburetor and for all future rights to manufacture them. This transaction resulted in the carburetor languishing, hidden away in a safe at the corporate headquarters of a giant oil conglomerate.

A few years later, as a college student who had by now heard four or five versions of the tale, I began to have some doubts. After learning a thing or two about thermodynamics in physics classes, my doubts escalated to the level where I began to think of the story as "The Legend of the Magic Carburetor." The characters and locations cited in the many carburetor legends I have encountered have been quite varied. Many were told to me by my students, and I must have encountered at least a dozen different versions of the tale over the past fifty years.

In one version, there was this race car builder in North Carolina who invented the magic carburetor, and a couple of sinister fellows came all the way up from Texas to make him an offer that he could not refuse. In another version, a professor at Georgia Tech was the legendary inventor. He drove his car with its magic carburetor to campus every day, until an agent of General Motors bought the car, carburetor and all, for an astronomical sum of money.

The magic carburetor myth may have originated in Toronto, about 1935, where the inventor of the allegedly superefficient *Pogue Carburetor* claimed it was being crushed by a corporate conspiracy. Or it may have originated in Daytona in the 1960's, where the *Fish Carburetor* supposedly suffered a similar fate. Both of these carburetors were actually manufactured and sold, but neither came close to the performance claimed by their promoters.

For anyone unfamiliar with the term, a *carburetor* is (or was) the more-or-less complicated, pot-shaped thingy that used to sit on top of automobile engines and introduce vaporized fuel into their fiery internal workings. A carburetor of one form or another was used on most gasoline-fueled automobile engines for almost a century. Then, about two decades ago, it began to be replaced by more efficient and reliable *fuel injection*. Modern fuel injection is a computer controlled delivery system which precisely "sprays" the required amount of fuel into the combustion chambers of the engine under very high pressure.

Now that the carburetor has been replaced by fuel injection on every new production model automobile available in the United States, one might expect the magic carburetor myth to be defunct. That certainly was my assumption until just recently, when a well-educated friend of mine confided an updated version of the legend to me, as sincerely as though he was sharing the gospel. A check of the Internet quickly revealed the magic carburetor myth to be alive and well.

Most conspiracy stories which revolve about the alleged suppression of technological secrets have the same fundamental problem – scientific principles are universal. By that I mean that whatever one company discovers, other companies will soon know also. (As an example of this principle, legend has it that the "secret formula" for Coca Cola is kept in a heavily guarded safe at the company headquarters in Atlanta. The reality is that any competent analytical chemist could purchase a bottle of Coke and determine the precise amount of every ingredient in a matter of a few hours.) Even authoritarian governments that wish to restrict the spread of the new scientific discoveries have trouble doing so.

The fuel mileage allegedly produced by the magic carburetor varies somewhat from one version of the legend to another, but they all claim to have delivered fuel mileage which is literally incredible for a conventional passenger car. On the other hand, the maximum fuel mileage which can be achieved by a vehicle designed with fuel mileage as the only objective is virtually unlimited.

A few years ago, a gasoline fuel mileage record was set by a three-wheeled, carbon fiber car weighing 65 pounds, driven by an 85 pound woman lying flat on her back. The car was powered by an intermittently-operating, internal-combustion engine the size of a beer can. The mileage attained by this car, while cruising around an indoor track at a speed of 25 mi/hr, was in excess of 2,400 miles per gallon. Attaining 2,400 mi per gal (also expressed as 2,400 MPG or 2,400 mi/gal) is truly an impressive performance, even for an experimental vehicle such as the one just described. Useful things are surely learned through this sort of exercise, but such exotic automobiles do have a rather limited utility for tasks such as transporting the kids to school and hauling home the groceries.

According to Guinness, the current World Record for the fuel mileage obtained by a production model gasoline powered passenger automobile while operating under actual road conditions is 64.4 miles per gallon. This was achieved by a husband and wife team driving 2012 Chevrolet Cruze ECO over a distance of some 9,500 miles. (I assume that the husband was unwilling to stop and ask directions.) This is a respectable accomplishment to be sure, but these are professionals, driving over a computer-selected route which avoided steep inclines, high speed freeways, and traffic snarls.

But is it not also possible that some kind of radical new design of carburetor, transmission, or other innovation, could result in an automobile which can achieve such fuel mileage for ordinary people driving their ordinary cars in their daily commutes? The short answer is no, but the logical way to begin analyzing the question is by considering the amount of energy which can actually be obtained by burning a gallon of gasoline. If you will trust me to provide you with accurate numbers, I can spare you most of the boring mathematics.

An energy unit familiar to most of us is the kilowatt-hour, the same energy unit used by the electric power company on our energy bills. The complete burning of one gallon of gasoline releases 36 kilowatt-hours of energy. This is a quantity of energy not too different from the amount of electrical energy which, on the average, each American uses in one day. Three-fourths of one kilowatt is about equal to one horsepower, making 48 horsepower-hours another way of describing the amount of energy in a gallon of gasoline. So how far can the 48 horsepower-hours of energy move an automobile? The short answer is, "it depends," but the maximum distance possible depends on just a few basic factors.

The motion of a car along a level road is mainly opposed by two forces: the resistance of the tires rolling over the road and the wind resistance of the car moving through the air. The amount of tire resistance drag depends mostly on the weight of the car, while the amount of air resistance drag depends on the shape of the car and its speed.

A mid-sized car, such as an older Ford Taurus or a Toyota Camry, moving at a speed of 60 miles per hour along smooth, level pavement, typically must overcome about 50 pounds of tire drag and 100 pounds of air resistance. The power required to overcome the total resistance of 150 pounds while moving at 60 mi/hr is about 24 horsepower. If all of the combustion energy of the fuel could be applied to moving the car, the 48 horsepower-hours contained in one gallon of gasoline would propel a car for a distance of about 120 miles at a constant speed of 60 mi/hr along a smooth, level roadway. Most of us would be delighted with 120 mi/gal, but unfortunately, as we drive along at 60 mi/hr, more of the energy released by burning the fuel goes out through the radiator and the exhaust pipe than is actually used to move the car.

The efficiency of the gasoline-fueled automobile engine has been stuck on about 30 percent for several years now. This level of efficiency could mean that if you are driving across Nebraska at a constant 60 mi/hr in a mid-sized car, you would expect a fuel mileage of a little less than 30% of 120 mi/gal or about 36 mi/gal. But there are a few more considerations.

A little energy is used by the alternator, a little more by the air conditioner, some is lost in the transmission, etc. In nice, round numbers, a reasonable fuel-mileage expectation might be about 30 mi/gal. It is possible that you might sometimes get a little better mileage due to helpful factors such as a good tail wind, but in the real world, where you will probably have to make a stop or two and accelerate to pass a few times, the gas mileage is likely to be somewhat less. If you tell me that your Taurus gets 30 mi/gal on the highway, I will have little reason to doubt you. If you claim 50 mi/gal, however, even in Nebraska, I may question either your arithmetic or your character.

Is it possible that the efficiency of the gasoline engine will be significantly improved? The theoretical maximum efficiency of any internal combustion engine depends on how hot the fuel burns compared to the coolness of the exhaust it emits. A calculation based on this principle (the second law of thermodynamics) gives the modern gasoline engine a theoretical maximum efficiency of about 55 percent. (Diesel engines are somewhat more efficient than gasoline fueled engines because diesel fuel is burned at a higher temperature.)

If your car was equipped with a carburetor or an injection system which would enable the engine to achieve this theoretical maximum of 55 percent efficiency, then you could perhaps get 50 mi/gal while driving across Nebraska at 60 mi/hr, but still no 200 miles per gallon. I doubt that a "conventional" gasoline powered automobile, the size and weight of a Taurus or a Camry and traveling at highway speeds, will ever attain a gasoline mileage that very much exceeds 40 mi/gal. To do so would violate the laws of thermodynamics, and for one who believes the laws of thermodynamics to be correct, the only explanation for the claim of a 200 MPG carburetor is either magic or delusion.

The amount of petroleum in the earth and its availability for our future use are subjects of considerable debate. On a time scale of a few generations, however, it is definitely a finite resource. Most of us want to make petroleum fuel last as long as possible, and many of us would prefer not to go to war to obtain more of it. Global warming is also a concern, and hybrid car technology is only a small part of the solution. But for individuals who wish to reduce their own automotive fuel consumption right away, the options are, in order of feasibility: (1) drive slower, (2) drive less, (3) drive smaller, or (4) drive a diesel or a hybrid. Not even a law passed by Congress and signed by the President of the United States will make the internal combustion gasoline-fueled engine a great deal more efficient, or result in the creation (or even the evolution) of a magic carburetor.

One evening not long ago, while relaxing at a favorite watering hole, some friends and I were lamenting the resurgence of the 200 mile per gallon carburetor legend. A burly patron who was seated nearby overheard our conversation and loudly informed us that his daddy was a good friend of the inventor of the 200 MPG carburetor. He then ominously wanted to know if we thought his daddy was a liar. The Magic Carburetor Myth can even be hazardous to your health.

Any sufficiently advanced technology is indistinguishable from magic.
—Arthur C. Clarke

The Day I Fell off the Turnip Truck

"Hey Mack, wanna to go to the beach?" Bill, the chubby guy from across the hall came trotting into my dormitory room. "Grab your stuff and let's go to the beach!"

"Go to the beach? Had he lost his mind?" Here it is, a Thursday morning in Boone, North Carolina, about 300 miles from the coast. I have eight dollars and thirty cents in my pocket, a chemistry lab at 2:00, three Friday classes, and with no advance warning, some nut wants to know if I want to go to the beach. Well, why not?

I had not been in North Carolina long, but one thing I had already learned; when folks in that part of the state said "The Beach," they invariably meant Myrtle Beach, South Carolina. Strange as it seemed at the time, Myrtle Beach is the nearest access to the east coast from Boone, North Carolina.

Although it was a chilly, drizzly, May day in the North Carolina mountains, Bill was assuring everyone that it would be clear and balmy at Myrtle Beach. I don't know where he got his information, but he was very convincing.

Bill was an upperclassman and a veteran who owned his own car. I was surprised that he was asking me, a freshman, if I wanted to go the beach. He rattled off his beach trip presentation like a Vegematic salesman. "I know a bunch of girls from up here who have a house rented at the beach for the weekend. We will have a free place to sleep and party. These are really cool gals. Hey, Mack, even you might get lucky. I'll drive my car if you guys will buy the gas."

There were a lot of reasons why it took a while for Bill to convince me to go. "At least five bucks for gas. What about food? What about beer? What about my Friday classes? But what the heck, if I can borrow twenty bucks from somebody, count me in. I'll go." My roommate, Wayne, who really wanted to go, loaned me twenty bucks with the understanding that I would influence Bill to include him in the trip. Wayne was the fifth and final member of the party of ASTC students who were on our way from Boone to Myrtle Beach. We were out on a grand adventure indeed, I thought. I had only seen the ocean once before and that was at Virginia Beach when I went to 4H camp. Myrtle Beach is not like 4H camp, I was told.

By noon, the five of us were all squeezed into Bill's 1951 Plymouth and making our way through the fog, winding over Route 321 toward Blowing Rock. Before we were even headed down the mountain, the subject arose concerning what we should provide in the way of food and drink in return for the hospitality of our hostesses. The veteran beach goers immediately declared that P.J. was essential for any beach party, especially if there was going to be a lot of shagging. Up until that time, the term "shagging" had always had a somewhat different meaning in my experience, but I didn't have to listen too long before I realized that the guys were actually talking about dancing. Everyone else soon agreed that P.J. was to be the preferred beverage, a decision made without my participation. Prior to that conversation, I had never heard of either a dance called "The shag" or a drink called "P.J." When I innocently asked what P.J. stood for, one guy declared that it was for "Purple

Jesus," but another disagreed, declaring that it was simply short for "Purple Juice." Either way, I felt that P.J. would be an essential part of my education.

Two members of our expedition began insisting that we must take a route that would go through Charlotte. That would be so we could swing by Tanner's Hot Dog Stand uptown to buy some of the famous Tanner's Punch. "That's the stuff you really have to have to mix up really good PJ, Tom from Charlotte insisted. "It makes it easy to fix, and it is really good. The great thing about Tanner's Punch is you can't taste the booze in it at all." Then he added. "Bill, if you'll take us through Charlotte, I'll buy the punch. Right through uptown is the best route to Myrtle Beach anyway."

"Just tell me where to turn," conceded Bill. Less than three hours later we were driving up West Trade Street to uptown Charlotte.

This was my first time ever in Charlotte, North Carolina, and it looked like a really big city to me. A couple of the buildings must have been at least ten or twelve stories high. I thought the tall structure with ACC emblazoned all around the top must be the headquarters of the Atlantic Coast (athletic) Conference, but I was quickly informed that the building housed a large bank, the Atlantic Credit Corporation. But the traffic impressed me most. I thought it positively frightening.

When we stopped at a traffic light at the intersection of Tryon and Trade Streets, I was informed that we were now at "The Square." Tom and Wayne jumped out of the car and ran up Tryon Street toward a little nondescript store front. The large sign above the door said "TANNERS" in huge orange letters. If not for the pyramids of oranges in the window, I would have never guessed that the store sold a famous recipe fruit punch. Bill circled a long block, while Augie, another provincial Charlottean, called out what he considered to be the major points of interest. First he directed my attention to The National Hat Shop, where he said one should go if they wanted to buy hockey tickets. Go figure. He then pointed out such landmarks as The Independence Building, Izzy Pittles Delicatessen, and First Presbyterian Church, but none of these icons had a great deal of meaning for me.

When we drove back down the street to the front of Tanners, Bill pulled over to the curb to where Tom and Wayne, each carrying two one-gallon jugs of a purple liquid, were waiting. Four gallons of punch! Funny how quickly these things get out of hand.

As we drove down South Tryon Street, a discussion began between Augie and Tom concerning the most convenient location of a liquor store. This was followed by a poll to determine just who in the car was at least twenty-one years old. As it turned out, Bill and Tom were also the only ones of the group whose ages exceeded the magical number required to legally buy hard liquor in North Carolina. Tom directed Bill as he drove down East Morehead Street almost to King's Drive, the location of a North Carolina ABC store.

I thought it strange that there was no discussion at all about the kind of booze that was going to be bought, but apparently everyone in the car but me knew all of the ingredients required for PJ. When Bill came out of the ABC store with several pints of something labeled Everclear, the other guys cheered. I innocently commented that did not look like a lot of booze for the five of us, our hostesses, and whomever else might show up for the party that was sure to happen. It was then that I was informed that Everclear was absolute ethanol, 190 proof grain alcohol, powerful enough to be fatal if not sufficiently diluted with a proper buffering agent such as Tanner's Punch. The basic recipe called for one pint of Everclear to one gallon of punch, I was told. That was a concentration at which the alcohol allegedly could not even be tasted. But Tom declared that two pints of Everclear to one gallon of punch was the proportion required to give PJ its certifiable properties as an aphrodisiac.

When I pointed out that the label clearly warned *For industrial purposes only!*, my friends were reassuring. "Oh, don't worry about that," I was told. "People drink this stuff all the time. They wouldn't sell it in the ABC store of it wasn't okay. Don't worry about it."

From Morehead and Kings, we wound our way through a maze of different Queen's Roads while looking for Highway 16 and somehow ended up headed east on a major thoroughfare called Independence Boulevard, also labeled as US Route 74. To our great relief, Augie declared route 74 to be the first leg of the speediest route from Charlotte to Myrtle Beach, South Carolina.

As we drove east along Independence, we suddenly came upon a large structure of such an unusual form that my first thought was that it must be a crashed flying saucer. It was then that Augie proudly pointed out the odd building to the rest of us as the new Charlotte Coliseum, where, if you got your tickets from the National Hat Shop, you could go to an ice hockey game. What a strange town, I was thinking.

From the Charlotte Coliseum we eased on down Highway 74 to Monroe, where we eventually encountered Highway 601. When Bill announced that he now knew where we were, and that we were officially on our way to Myrtle Beach, everyone cheered.

We had not escaped from Boone until sometime in the afternoon. With the combination of rural Carolina roads, the stopping and shopping in Charlotte, and some misunderstanding of the less-than-precise directions to our destination, it was almost nine p.m. before we located the house where we were supposed to stay. It was near, but not at, Myrtle Beach. All but two of the girls from Appalachian were off somewhere enjoying the Myrtle Beach night life. They were all at a place called the "Pad," I think someone said.

The house, three rows back from the beach, was rambling, weathered, and dilapidated. It appeared to have four small bedrooms, a spacious living area with lots of wicker sofas and chairs, and a bar separating the living area from the kitchen. There were screened-in porches in the front and the back, and it was soon pointed out to me that my sleeping facilities consisted of a chaise lounge on the front porch. Not a padded or upholstered chaise lounge, mind you, but a folding contraption made of aluminum tubing and woven plastic bands, the kind then available at Atlantic Mills Discount Mart for about five bucks. Luckily, I had the foresight to bring my own blanket.

Before turning in, we all walked down to the Board-walk for hotdogs and beer. The legal age for purchasing beer in South Carolina was eighteen back then, which was fortunate for me, since I survived almost entirely on hotdogs and draft beer for the whole weekend. Enough beer, even beer which is 3.2 percent alcohol, can make it possible for one to sleep on a fold-ing chaise lounge. But then one does have to get up a lot during the night.

We arose quite early on Friday. It was important that we have sufficient time to engage in all of the essential beach activ-ities: getting sunburned, stepping on sand burrs, buying stupid hats, drinking more beer and eating more hotdogs, and looking at the girls. I do believe that we spent more of our time looking than any of the other essential activities.

Early on Friday afternoon, we had our unfortunate in-troduction to the arcane Myrtle Beach legal system. Augie spotted someone he knew out on the Boardwalk and stepped out of the Arcade with a beer in his hand. He was immediately accosted by a Myrtle Beach Police Officer and given a citation. Then we had to pass the hat to gather enough money to pay the $26.00 fine required to keep Augie from spending the night in jail. This was an unanticipated expense which left us all a bit short of beer and hot dog money.

Since the activity was essentially free, we spent the rest of the afternoon hanging out with other guys who also appeared to be seriously engaged in girl watching. When some of the girls appeared to be watching us right back, Bill warned us that, since we were only guests in the house where we were staying, we must not let any of them follow us home, chortle, chortle. (Remember, this was at the beach and in the fifties, and PC was still considered less important than PJ.)

When we finally returned to the house on late Friday afternoon, a group of partiers had already begun to gather. We made our contribution to the festivities by quickly mixing up a big batch of PJ. Someone put a Maurice Williams record on the stereo, turned it way up loud, and the mating rituals began in earnest. It wasn't long before the party expanded outside, so Augie and Bill went around the yard, warning everyone outside that any consumption of alcohol must take place on the property and preferably inside. They should know.

I felt out of place at first, not knowing many of the people there. The guys I had ridden to the beach with and the two girls from Appalachian, whom I had just met briefly, were lost in the crowd and I was on my own. After dancing with a couple of strange girls (take that any way you want) and engaging in a few attempts to converse with folks I didn't know over deafening music, I just dipped myself a Dixie Cup of PJ, went out onto my front porch suite, and sunk down into my chase lounge. This stuff is pretty good, I thought as I took my first-ever sip of PJ. Then I laid back, pulled my stupid hat down over my eyes and lay there listening to the party noise and the beach music. I was just "cooling it," to use the phrase of the day.

I must have drifted off, because I sat up with a start when I felt another body drop down on the lounge beside me. As I pushed my hat up out of my face, I heard this very southern voice saying to me, "Well, heigh theah. Who are you?"

There, sitting near the foot of the lounge was this very sophisticated looking young woman. She was wearing a red flowered sun dress which perfectly complimented her golden tan and streaked blonde hair. She looked vaguely familiar to me, but I assumed that was only because she looked like she had just stepped down from the Hawaiian Tropic billboard out on Highway 17. There she was, just sitting with me on the chaise, smiling like a dream come true, and sipping on a cup of something, probably PJ. "I'll bet this is why guys come to the beach," I thought.

"I'm Mack. And who might you be?" I was trying so very hard to be cool.

"I'm Judy. Hey, this is the best PJ I have ever tasted."

"It's from an old family recipe," I assured her, still struggling to be cool and clever. Since I thought that a lot of the girls at the party were not from Appalachian, my first attempt at conversation was to ask her where she went to school

"Oh, I'm in premed at Duke," she sniffed, with a toss of her streaked tresses. "How about you?"

I was tempted to lie, but I knew that with a snoot full of PJ, if I even tried shooting a line of bull, I would screw up any creative claims I might dream up. I just told it like it was. "Oh, I'm just a Boone Goon," I replied, making light of my lowly status.

For a moment she looked puzzled, then the light dawned. "Oh, Appalachian State Teachers College. I thought I heard her place a demeaning emphasis on the word "Teachers," as she continued her critique. "Well, I think Boone is just about the most Godforsaken place I have ever seen," she unloaded on me. "Why on earth would anyone go to school there if they could possibly get in any place else?"

Wow! I guess now I knew where I stood. One can only respond to a statement like that by either becoming defensive or deflecting it with humor.

"I almost went to Duke," I claimed.

"Oh, really?" Her response was quite chilly.

"Yeah. I could have gone on a scholarship if I had scored 400 points higher on the College Boards or grown a foot and a half taller." She seemed to think that was funny, and our pleasant conversation continued.

She soon informed me that she was from Charlotte, had gone to Myers Park High School, and had come to the party because she was a friend of some of the App girls. Having taken a quickie tour of the town the day before, I was able to act as though I knew all about the sights and scenes of Charlotte.

After we chatted for a while, danced a little, and each drunk another cup of PJ, the alleged properties of the drink began to have their effect on me. I felt obligated to engage in some of the adventures people said often occurred at the beach, so I started nuzzling Miss Judy as we danced and even managed to maneuver her out of the living area and into one of the bed rooms. We wrestled on the bed for a while, engaging in some pretty heavy making out. But just as I began to "get down to the basics," as they say, Judy pushed me away and sat up. "Do you have any protection?"

"Protection?" The PJ must have addled my mind.

"Protection! A condom, stupid! Did you just fall off the turnip truck?"

I desperately tried to think how I could make the embarrassing admission that I did not have protection. I was feeling that I really had just fallen off the turnip truck, when someone began twisting the door knob and then rapped sharply on the door.

Then there came a voice from the other side. "Judy, are you in there? Are you alright?"

"Who in the world?" I wondered.

"I'm alright Mrs. Simpkins. I'm just lying down for a few minutes. I have a headache." Judy lied most convincingly, I thought.

"Well, some of your friends are looking for you. I think you had better come on out right away." It was obvious that the voice from the other side was not being fooled.

"Who in the hell is Mrs. Simpkins?" I whispered to Judy.

"She is our fellowship counselor," was her reply.

"Your fellowship counselor? What kind of fellowship counselor?"

"As in the Westminster Fellowship. Don't you know anything? This house belongs to the Methodist Church. I'm down here with the Westminster Fellowship girls from our church."

Oh, good grief! Here I was in the bedroom of a house that belonged to the Methodist Church, making out with one of

their fellowship girls, a Methodist girl whom I had been providing with large quantities of PJ. There had to be some severe
penalty for being that stupid!

"Are you in trouble," I asked, "caught drinking PJ, and
all that?"

"I don't think so. Mrs. Simpkins is a pretty cool lady.
She just wants to make sure nobody gets knocked-up. She
wouldn't know PJ from Kool-Aid, but I think we had better get
out of here. She will definitely be right back."

As Judy stood up and straightened out her clothes, she
acted kind of pissed, but I didn't know if she was mad at me or
just mad about the situation. As she exited the room, she found
it necessary to make a dramatic pause in the doorway. Then
with a toss of her streaked hair and a tilt of her nose, she made
her disappearance, slamming the door behind her.

I just sat there for a minute, feeling stupid and incompetent and guilty. It was not so much for not getting it on with
the girl of my dreams, but I felt that I was one of the persons responsible for converting a church outing into something resem-
bling a frat party. But dammit, Bill didn't say anything about
any Westminster Fellowship. How was I supposed to know that
we were screwing around with Methodist girls and giving them
liquor to boot? I should have been thankful that it wasn't a Baptist group, I suppose, with all that dancing going on.

A couple poked their heads in to the room, checking
to see if it was occupied, I guessed. I went back out to join the
festivities, but Miss Judy was nowhere to be seen.

The place was packed full, and the noise, with the music and the shagging and the yakking, and some idiots singing along off-key, was simply overwhelming. As I looked around, I spotted this rather tall, dignified looking, grey haired woman, who was just wandering around, watching as though she was keeping an eye on things. I was sure that this attractive older lady must be Mrs. Simpkins. As I watched her watching the partiers, she walked into the kitchen area and approached the bowl of PJ. To my horror, she dipped herself a cup, sniffed it, and then tasted it. I was holding my breath as Mrs. Simpkins made an awful face and then looked seriously down into her cup. But then she turned her cup up and drank it down. I was wondering if she could taste the Everclear, when she dipped into the bowl and poured herself a refill. Mrs. Simpkins then left the kitchen, walking right past me and giving a wicked wink as she brushed by. She continued to carry her cup as she made the rounds, still keeping an eagle eye on her Westminster Fellowship Girls.

"That is one cool lady," I thought, as she disappeared into the crowd. A while later Mrs. Simpkins came walking back by, and darned if she didn't go into the kitchen and get herself a PJ refill. As I stood there at the door to the kitchen, she walked past me and into one of the bed rooms, carrying her cup and moving a bit unsteadily. She closed the door behind her, the lock clicked, and that was the last I saw of Mrs. Simpkins that evening.

I was pretty well potted at this point, but I stupidly poured myself another cup of PJ anyway, and went out onto the front porch. Not much was happening out there, so I flopped down on my lounge and must have gone to sleep.

The next thing I knew, the bright sun was glaring in my face, but I wasn't sure where I was. When I tried to sit up, I couldn't move, and I was instantly in a panic. My first thought was that I had been poisoned by the Everclear. I seemed to be paralyzed! I couldn't budge, I felt numb, and I was suffocating! My head was throbbing, I couldn't breathe, and my mouth felt like it was stuffed with octopus tentacles. Have you ever had a dream where you are trying to run or call for help, but you can't move or make a sound? That's how it was right then, only it wasn't a dream. I really could not move and I really was smothering. When I did finally summon the strength to sit up and yell, a tangled and streaked mass of blonde hair popped up in front of my face and suddenly I could breathe. And there was Judy, wedged into the lounge chair, half beside and half on top of me, looking like she felt about as bad as I did.

"Oh! Mack! Sorry, I guess I crashed," she mumbled, as she squeezed out from between me and the arm of the lounge. "I got to feeling really sick last night, and I had to lie down someplace. Then I saw you out here and I thought you were somebody I could trust. Are you all right?"

"Oh, I'm okay," I lied. "We were just squeezed in here so tight that I was having trouble breathing. And actually, I do feel terrible."

"Me too, I feel just awful," she admitted, as she pusher her hair back and followed her admission by an avowal. "I am never going to drink that PJ stuff again."

"Me neither. Never again," I responded. Bad as we felt,

we both had to laugh as it occurred to us both, just how often that vow must have been repeated under similar circumstances.

"Oh God, I gotta go potty," Judy announced indelicately, struggling to her feet and almost falling over a trash can which had been placed right beside the lounge chair. It was a receptacle into which someone, probably she or I or both of us, had copiously barfed. As she headed into the house, she paused at the door, then turned and expelled a quick admission, as though the words all tasted bad.

"I have to tell you the truth, Mack. I'm not really a Dookie. Actually, I'm a Happy Appy too, just like you." Her lovely head she then bowed in sincere contrition.

"That's OK," I assured her, as I struggled to maintain my cool facade. "Everybody lies at the beach."

Last night I had already figured out that she wasn't from Duke. If she was, why would she be here with a bunch of girls from the Boone Methodist Church's Westminster Fellowship? I was really glad she had leveled with me, and really happy to learn that she was an Appalachian student. The future could hold all kinds of possibilities, I imagined, if we both ever got safely back to Boone.

"And I'm not from Charlotte either," she said even more quickly. "I'm from Hudson."

"That's okay too," I assured her, then wisely repeated, "Everybody lies at the beach. And Hudson is a real neat place." Now I was dispensing worldly wisdom, but if I hadn't ridden from Boone to Charlotte two days before, I would not have even known there was a Hudson, North Carolina.

"Well, I'm glad you didn't lie," Judy told me. "When I first saw you last night, I was pretty sure I had seen you on campus." Sometimes it pays to play it straight.

"Well, is Judy your real name?" I didn't really mean for the question sound like a dig, but she quickly became defensive.

"Of course it is. My name is Judy Sinclair, I'm from Hudson, North Carolina, and I'm a history major at Appalachian State Teachers College. Now, is there anything else you would like to know?"

"Well, there is just one more little thing. Did we do anything major last night?" I felt really stupid, having to ask.

Judy just rolled her eyes, then marched back across the porch and planted herself right in front of me. Then she took my face in her hands and looked into my eyes with a scowl.

"Listen sweet pea," she sternly lectured. "If we had done anything major last night, you wouldn't have to ask, you'd remember. Besides, I was worried most of the night that you were actually dead."

"Well, okay. But can I tell the guys that I slept with Judy Sinclair on the chaise lounge last night. That would be all right, wouldn't it?" I was teasing of course.

"If you tell anybody about us sleeping on that lounge, you had darn-well better tell them that all we did was sleep, or I will kill you." As she gave me her un-amused reply, she turned and bolted into the house.

As Judy disappeared, the porch began spinning and I had to lie back down. Then, as I needed the trash can again, I thought that I might be going to die. Later, I had the comforting thought that, if I lived through the day, maybe I would see Judy again that night. Sometimes you just have to find the strength to go on.

Epilogue: I have never even considered taking a drink of PJ since that day. For years afterward, even the mention of the stuff would make my stomach churn. Everyone I have heard mention PJ since that time usually concluded their discussion with the same declaration: "God, that stuff made me sick as a dog, and I have never tasted it again." Perhaps Everclear really is an industrial chemical.

Experience enables you to recognize a mistake when you make it again.

—Franklin P. Jones

Miss January

If it had been possible to Google the word *pompous* in nineteen fifty-eight, the image that popped up would surely been Dr. Jonathan Jacobs. He was not a very old man, probably in his early fifties, but his appearance was one of great age and wisdom. Bald, rotund, and sleepy-eyed, he must have surely been aware of his amazing resemblance to the Buddha, had the Buddha been attired as a funeral director and worn round steel-rimmed spectacles. Although it was told that this assistant professor of history at Appalachian State Teachers College had never completed his doctorate, that did not matter to his students. His manner was so professionial that we chose to call him *Doctor* Jacobs anyway. It did not take too many sessions of his World History lectures, however, for his aura of great wisdom to be dispelled.

Professor Jacobs would always arrive for his 9:00 am American History class precisely at 8:55 am, making a grand entrance into the classroom. After walking slowly and rigidly to the lectern (which rather resembled a pulpit), he would slowly extract his black roll book from the depths of an ancient leather flap-over briefcase. The ritual never varied; he would lick his thumb, leaf through his roll book to the appropriate class, clear his throat, inhale deeply, and begin calling the roll. He could make the roll call sound like some sonorous religious incantation, and if you arrived after your name had been called, then it was just too bad for you. Upon completion of the roll call, the black book was plunged back into the depths of his briefcase, from which it could never be extracted for the benefit of any late arrivals. The class was rather large, about forty students as I recall, and since the roll was always called alphabetically, student Brad Zakowsky could actually sleep about five minutes later in the mornings than Ed Abernathy. Ed often complained about the unfairness of it all.

The professor never looked up while calling the roll, so a student could answer for a friend who was not there. That was something that frequently happened, but the professor always appeared to remain completely unaware.

Once the task of calling the roll was behind him, Dr. Jacobs would slowly look around the room to insure everything was in its proper order; if his specifications were met, he would then place a stack of yellowed notes on the lectern, leaf through them until he found where he ended the last lecture, and begin to drone.

At the start of the Fall Term, Dr. Jacobs gave the class a parallel reading list, from which I selected a book published as one of the Time-Life History Series. I can't remember the name of the book, but it was about the American Revolution. When I turned in an index card synopsis of my reading, as we were required to do weekly, he called me out in class for listing a magazine article as parallel reading. A magazine article, he said, was not acceptable. When I attempted to explain that the Time Life Publication I had read was a book, not a magazine article, he became quite angry and defensive. The man did not even know what was on his own reading list.

Although Dr. Jacobs read from his notes throughout

most of the first term, in the second term, he simply read selected passages from the textbook. When some of the students
caught on and began following him in their own texts and un-
derlining those passages, he commanded that they must stop
that immediately. He told the students that it was necessary for
to write down notes about what he was reading for them to truly
learn the material.

The classroom used for Prof. Jacobs' history class must
have also been used for geography classes. There were racks
of retractable maps mounted along the tops of the large chalk
boards that ran all across the front and down one side of the
room. Whatever the room was used for prior to our history
class, there would always be several maps hanging down in
front of the boards. I never recall Professor Jacobs writing a
word on those chalkboards, but the maps left hanging in front
of the boards appeared to be a great affront to him.

Whenever the professor would walk into the room and
find maps which had not been retracted, he would heave a huge
sigh of frustration and shake his head in disgust, as if to say,
"the barbarians have been at it again." He would walk along the
boards retracting the maps, one by one, from the left front of
the room to the right rear, mumbling to himself the whole time.
The hanging map exercise appeared so frustrating to Dr. Jacobs
that certain students began arriving at the classroom early, just
in case there were no maps left down. If there were none, they
could always accommodate him by pulling down a few and
leaving them for him to retract. For the record, I was not one of
those guilty of harassing the poor professor.

One morning, however, Dr. Jacobs arrived to find that there had been just one map left down. A map of the Southeastern United States extended down to the level of the chalk tray, and it just happened to be covering the chalkboard at precisely the front and center of the class room.

The presence of the single map merited just a moderate sigh of frustration from the professor. He marched across the front of the room with his usual pompous dignity and just casually yanked down on the bottom of the map as he walked by, quickly releasing it. His casualness had it price though, for the dowel on the bottom of the map slipped from his fingers as soon as the catch was tripped, and the map zipped up the board and flipped over the top of the map rack, well beyond the reach of his pudgy fingers.

When the map retracted, it exposed a picture which had been securely taped to the center of the chalkboard. Dr. Jacobs aborted his promenade across the front of the room with a classic double take. The picture just revealed was the **Playmate of the Month,** the full color centerfold from the January issue of Playboy Magazine, now displayed before the class in all her strategic nudity. As the professor gasped and his face flushed to a deep crimson, he awkwardly pivoted so his back was to the board directly in front of the centerfold. He stood paralyzed there in front of the board with his arms spread wide in a cruciform stance, as though he considered it his duty to conceal this vision of loveliness from the eyes of his innocent students.

It must have soon occurred to him how ridiculous he appeared, because he turned toward the board and began making futile lurches to retrieve the map that had just retracted. It remained far beyond his reach, however, and it never occurred to him that he could have concealed the pinup by pulling down one of the other maps mounted lower in the same rack.

Finally, the frustrated professor attacked the image of the Playmate, ripping the nude photo from the board and crushing it into a small ball of compressed paper and stuffing it into the trash can in the corner of the room. He then returned to the board and carefully peeled the taped corners from the surface of the chalk board, taking care that not the tiniest scrap of the offending image should remain. He appeared to be engaged in a ritual of decontamination.

His frustration fully vented, Professor Jacobs recovered from the distraction, proceeded to the podium, and proceeded with his dreadfully dull lecture as though nothing had happened.

There was only one change in the professor's morning ritual following the incident. No matter how many maps were found to have been left hanging in front of the chalkboards when the professor arrived, they were allowed to remain just as he found them. But I did see him peek furtively around the edge of a map left hanging at the center of the board as he was leaving the room one morning.

Alias Jesse James

You just don't know what to expect from May weather in Boone, North Carolina. Near the end of May of 1954, for example, the graduation processional marched into the gymnasium with an inch of snow on the graduates' mortar boards. The winter of 1959 had been an especially cold one, so when the first Saturday in May of that year turned out clear and balmy, students who had spent most of the winter hunkered down in their dorm rooms were ready to get out and find some kind of physical activity. In Boone, there is plenty of time to study when the weather is lousy.

The dorm I was living in that year, Justice Hall, was located near the top of a hill on the south side of campus. Looking out across the campus and the town from our fourth floor vantage point, Howard's Knob could be seen to the north of town, looming a thousand feet above it. The view from up there should be great on a day like this. "Hey guys, what do you say we hike up Howard's Knob?" someone suggested.

Nobody seemed to know much about Howard's Knob back then, whether it was private property, or even if there was a hiking trail to the top. From our view, we could see that just up the hill from the edge of town, there were cows grazing in a steep pasture. There were a couple of cabins on the ridge to the west of the knob and we could see a road zigzagging up the mountain to them. It looked like it shouldn't be too hard to get up to the top. Lance Reed was from nearby Lenoir, which practically made him a resident of Boone, and he said that he had heard that people hiked up there all the time.

That was good enough for us. There were two or three more besides Lance and myself, and at the last minute, Otie Benetti, griping and grousing as usual, decided he would join the group. There were at least half a dozen of us ASTC students who trooped out of Justice Hall and down the hill, toward the campus and the town of Boone.

Before we left, everyone but Otie grabbed a jacket. This was Boone, after all, and although the temperature was in the seventies right then, we all knew it could snow before we got back to campus. Otie, being from Buffalo, New York, told us that we were all a bunch of sissies and headed out on the hike with no jacket and wearing a short-sleeved tee shirt.

Otie was kind of a strange guy anyway. Not just because he was from up north, but also because he worked so hard at being a tough character. He really wasn't a bad guy, once you got to know him, but the first time I ever saw him I thought that he was about the meanest looking cuss I had ever seen. He had these beady black eyes, for one thing, and they continually shifted back and forth, beneath his one bushy eyebrow that extended continuously across his forehead. His enormous beak and substantial overbite combined to give him the appearance of a giant raptor.

Otie was pretty tall, maybe six-two, with extremely broad shoulders, but almost no neck. Whenever he was talking to someone, his height and his short neck caused him to cock his head to one side and look at them out of the corner of his eye. He always talked out of the corner of his mouth, like everything he said was some big sinister secret, and even his everyday speech was punctuated with profanity of a level that few of us had ever heard. A lot of folks considered him plumb scary.

As we were walking through town I asked Gerald, who knew Otie much better than I did, if Otie was his real name. "Is Otie a nickname for Otis?" I asked.

"Shhhh!" responded Gerald. "His real name's not Otis, it's Wiley. But don't ever call him that. He hates his real name."

"Then, how did he get the nick name 'Otie'?" I persisted.

Gerald lowered his voice another notch. "Otie is short for Coyote. It's a joke, as in Wiley E. Coyote. Get it? Don't you think he looks like Wiley Coyote? I heard that his nickname in high school was Coyote, not Otie."

It took me a minute, but when I finally made the connection, I thought, "Maybe that's what makes him so scary." In fact, he not only looked like Wiley Coyote, he even moved like the Coyote in the Roadrunner Cartoons. I have no idea where Gerald got his information, but I promised myself that I would never call Otie anything but Otie. I also thought that sometime later I might look him up in the year book to see if Gerald was putting me on.

The town residences ended near the foot of the knob, and the road we were following soon began zigzagging its way up the steep side of the mountain. Although no one knew who owned the land we would be crossing, we decided to abandon the road anyway, and we began making a shortcut straight up the side of the mountain. That trek became pretty strenuous for a bunch of guys who had been mostly sitting on their butts for the last six months, so we soon had to take a break. As we sat on some large boulders just short of the summit, just drinking in the incredible view, I heard this odd sound, a sound that seemed very strange for Boone. I thought I could hear the sound of a train whistle, a steam train whistle at that. It made no sense to me at first, but I searched the horizon in the apparent direction of the sound. Way off in the distance to the south of Boone and toward Blowing Rock, I could see a column of smoke. The smoke appeared to be coming from a moving object that was snaking its way around a distant hill. "There's no dang railroad in Boone," I was thinking, "especially no steam powered train." But before I could ask anyone, my question was answered.

"Well, it looks like they have fired up Tweetsie," Lance commented.

"What the hell is Tweetsie?" Otie asked exactly what the rest of us were wondering.

Lance knew all about Tweetsie and was happy to share his knowledge. "Oh, some fellows from Blowing Rock bought the old narrow gauge train that used to run into Boone from Johnson City, Tennessee. You can see a part of the track they built, coming around that hill way over there." Lance pointed in the direction I had just been looking. "It's a ride, a tourist attraction," he told us. "They say the train was owned by Gene Autrey for a few years before it was brought back here."

"Well damn, if it belonged to Gene Autrey, I gotta go ride it right now," Otie sarcastically injected.

"Is it just kids that ride that thing around that hill? Does it just go round and round the hill? Does it burn wood?" Everyone wanted to know more about Tweetsie.

"It's a coal burner. Mostly kiddies ride it, but their mommys and their daddys can ride it, too," Lance, our Tweetsie expert explained. "It first started running, on and off, a couple of years ago. But they really got it going last year. Now, they have put down more track and made the ride longer, and the developers are building a western town around the train station. I have heard that they are going to have Indians attacking the train, and even outlaws robbing it. All kinds of stuff like that."

"Real Indians?" Otie wanted to know.

"Yep, and real outlaws, too," Lance joked.

Then Lance shared some more really interesting information. "I've heard that they're going to hire a bunch of Appalachian guys to dress up like Indians and cowboys and outlaws and stuff like that. So if any of you guys are looking for a summer job…"

Lance didn't need to finish. Summer job! Everybody we knew needed a summer job! Who were "they," and where did we go to apply?

Then Lance added the clincher: "The man to see is probably Grover Robbins, the man who owns the Tweetsie business. He needs a bunch of people to work full-time for the summer, and he might need some people to work on the weekends for the rest of May."

Lance admitted that there was a very good reason he knew so much about Tweetsie; he had already been hired to work there, beginning Sunday morning, the very next day. The hike to the top of Howard's Knob was immediately aborted.

Everybody in the group was interested in a job at Tweetsie and Lance would be our contact. Forget the hike. In about an hour we were back at the dorm, busy talking Lance into hauling us down to Tweetsie to apply for a job. Lance, good fellow that he was, was soon driving a car full of us the short distance down Highway 321 toward Blowing Rock and to Tweetsie Railroad.

We pulled into the gravel parking lot just down the hill from a building that might pass for an old-time train station. Looking around the place, we soon found a guy overseeing some construction beside the tracks who looked as though he might know what was going on around there. "Did Tweetsie need any more outlaws or Indians?" The fellow wasn't Mr. Robbins. His name was Mike, but he knew all about Tweetsie and yes, they were planning to hire some more.

"Do any of you have social security numbers?" was Mike's first question after we asked him about jobs.

We all had our socials. Mike was looking us over when Mr. Robbins himself walked out of the station. "We've got some guys from the college who say they want to work here," Mike told him.

Mr. Robbins kind of laughed, gave us all quick glance, and counted heads. Then he paused for a minute, looked hard at Otie, and walked right over to him. "Do you have a black outfit? Any western duds?" he asked.

"Well uh, I got a black shirt...," Otie appeared to be thinking really hard, his beady eyes rolled up into his head. Finally he blurted out, "But I ain't got no black jeans. And I ain't got no damn cowboy hat. Or boots."

Mr. Robbins studied him a bit longer, then said, "That's okay. Here's what you need to do. When you get back to Boone, you go into Smitty's and tell them to fix you up with a black cowboy outfit. Tell them that I said to charge it to the Tweetsie account. You are going to be our Jesse James."

The rest of us were just standing around with our mouths hanging open as he turned and waved his hand dismissively in our direction. "All of you be here at eight o'clock tomorrow morning and you can be members of the James Gang or Indians or something. Mike will explain it all to you."

Mr. Robbins had a short conversation with Mike which we could not hear. Then he abruptly stalked back inside.

So that was it? We were all hired? Not that any of us were really surprised that Otie was hired to be Jesse James.

Now, I had no idea what Jesse James really looked like, although I was pretty sure that he did not look much like the Rory Calhoun version I once saw in a really bad movie. And I was equally sure that the real Jesse James did not have an up-state New York accent. But Otie really was just about the tough-est, meanest looking hombre any of us had ever seen. Were they trying to scare the kids on the train?

Mike told two of the guys that they were going to be Indians. He then told me and Lance that we were to be mem-bers of the "James Gang" and that we were going to help Otie rob the train. But what would this all involve? Would we be required to ride horses? Would we be carrying guns?

We soon found that there were going to be no horses involved and that Tweetsie would provide black pigtailed wigs and rubber tomahawks for the Indians. They would furnish big hats and six-shooters – complete with belts, holsters and blank cartridges – for the outlaws. We outlaws were instructed to wear jeans and western-looking shirts, if we had them. Any kind of pull-on leather boots would make the outfits better.

The "Indian" costumes were a bit more problematic. Each "Indian" was responsible for his own make up. Mike suggested they wear tee shirts with the sleeves and tail cut up to make them fringed. The tee shirts should not have any printing or logos on them, and shirts imprinted with "Property of ASTC Athletic Department" were specifically prohibited. Mike also mentioned that an old pair of khakis, also fringed to resemble deer skin, would be good pants to wear, should anyone have a pair they were willing to sacrifice. This was going to be more complicated than I first thought.

That Sunday morning we soon-to-be Tweetsie employees were all up at an early hour. Before we left, somebody banged on Otie's door to see if he was ready, but we got no response. We had to leave right then because Lance was leaving, and he was our transportation to our new jobs. I banged on Otie's door again, just to make sure he was awake, but all we got was silence.

We actually got out to Tweetsie much earlier than necessary; it was May, after all, and word was not yet widespread that Tweetsie was open for business. We were also informed that we would not be on the clock until the train had delivered us to our proper stations around on the other side of the hill.

I think us so-called outlaws and Indians must have looked pretty ratty that morning. The "Indians" had talked some coeds into giving them bright lipstick and blue eye shadow for war paint, which didn't look too bad. But the costumes they wore made them look like they were going to work at the car wash. Putting on the black wigs helped them look a little bit more believable, and when two more experienced "Indians" arrived there for work, they helped the apprentice renegades improve their costumes.

We outlaws could have passed for real rough, tough western hombres. With our plaid shirts, boots, and jeans, plus big hats and six-shooters, we looked the outlaws from any old grade-B movie. But where was Otie? Since we had no Otie, one of the ersatz Indians was told to put on a cowboy hat and wear the pair of holsters with the twin special ivory handled six-shooters normally reserved for Jesse James. He was going to be the Jesse James for that day.

The train carried us around the hill out and of sight from the station, stopping to let the Indians off at the site from which they were to attack. The outlaws were stationed at another site a little farther down the line. Tweetsie actually did not make its first actual paying passenger run until about ten, which was just fine with us. We were given minimum instructions on how to play our roles, so the first time out, we just made it up as we went. Part of the skit was for two of us there to steal the "payroll" from the strongbox on the train, but I am sure that we were not the least bit convincing. Not one kid I saw looked the least bit scared of the train robbers, and several of them fired their cap guns at us. What was needed was Otie performing as a really scary Jesse James.

We limped through two pitiful train robberies that morning, but I think our robbing routine would have been significantly improved by the third time the train came around. We were just discussing improvements that might be made in our performance, when we heard this crashing and thrashing coming up the hill and through the woods behind us. Behold, a hot, sweaty, and very angry black-clad cowboy came bursting out into the clearing!

It was Otie, carrying his brand-new cowboy hat, and mad as the dickens. He had overslept and could not be convinced that we had all tried very hard to wake him up. He had set out to hitchhike from Appalachian out to Tweetsie, but apparently, no one would give a ride to someone who looked like Otie, walking down Highway 321 dressed up like a cowboy. He claimed that he walked all of the way from campus to Tweetsie in his fancy new cowboy boots. Now, his feet were all blistered and he was thoroughly pissed. But he was ready to rob the train. "Just gimme my guns," he demanded of the substitute Jesse.

About half an hour later, when the train came around the bend, we could see that it was packed full of little kids. But Otie, still steaming, was not interested in the robbery scenario we had previously worked out. "I'm the leader of this gang," he commanded. "You guys follow me."

We flagged the train to a halt and climbed on board, Otie in the lead. As soon as he was inside the first car, Otie jerked out his six-guns and fired two blanks shots down toward the floor.

"Awright, you little piss ants," he bellowed in his New York accent. "I'm Jesse James, and dis is a Goddamn stick-up!" Most of the little kids hunkered down behind the seats, scared half to death, and some of them started to cry. We followed Otie through the cars, with him cussing and shooting all the way, finally jumping off the end of the train.

When the next train came around, a very upset Mike was on board. Instead of us robbing the train this trip, he directed Otie to transfer the fancy guns back to the substitute Jesse and to accompany him back to the station. The rest of us were to continue with our train robbing as before.

None of us had any doubt about what was happening. Of course, Otie was being fired. We wondered if he was going to have to walk all the way back to the dorm, still wearing those cowboy boots that blistered his feet.

At the end of that long first day, when we rode the train back to the station, we found Otie there, waiting for his ride back to campus. Apparently, all of us were expected to show up for work the next Saturday.

We didn't ask Otie a thing until we were all in Lance's car. Then the questions began: "Had he been fired? Was Mr. Robbins upset? Had anyone complained?"

The answers from Otie were, "Yes, some people had complained. Mike was upset – he didn't know about Mr. Robbins. No, he was not fired, but he had been reassigned."

"You know what they got me doin'?" Otie complained.

"I spent the whole damn afternoon out in the parking lot, asking folks if I could put these stupid bumper stickers on their cars. Mike thinks it'll be great promotion to have a cowboy puttin' bumper stickers on the customers' cars at Tweetsie."

"My job is gonna' be puttin' these stupid stickers that say **TWEETSIE R.R., Blowing Rock, North Carolina** on everybody's car! That's everybody that don't mind a Tweetsie sticker on their bumper. I'm supposed to ask permission first. While I am doing all that, Mike wants me to keep wearing these damn cowboy boots that are killing my feet!"

I always thought that eighty percent of success is just showing up.

— Woody Allen

The Tea Man Cometh

One Saturday I was invited to ride down to Mount Lowell with my friend Jerry to sample some his Mama's home cooking. When Jerry introduced his mother, Mildred, I couldn't help but smile, thinking about how much she looked like Jerry wearing a wig. That was except for Jerry being about six-two and his mama only about five-ten. But they probably weighed about the same. Jerry knew that everybody noticed how much he looked like his mama. "Yeh," he would say. "I sure do take after Mama's side of the family."

Jerry was always unabashedly talking about his family and his home town. He loved his folks and he loved the place where he grew up. Like so many in small southern towns, Jerry grew up in sight of the house where his mother was born and his grandmother still lived. Jerry might never have thought about going to college had he not been recruited to play football, but once he had the opportunity, he took it seriously.

In the years that I had known Jerry, he must have told me his entire family history, even the part about his parents getting married during World War II, with Jerry already well on the way. They got married while his father, Dave, was home on furlough, and right after a short honeymoon at Myrtle Beach, Dave was shipped overseas. Jerry was over a year old the first time that Dave saw him. Mildred was working at Stevens Denim Mills when they got married and kept on working there except for the two weeks she took off when Jerry was born. When the war ended and Dave came home in one piece, he immediately started to work at Steven's, too.

The mill was within walking distance of Mildred's mother's home, so with the housing shortage after the war, it just made sense for Dave and Mildred to move in with her. Mildred's parents, Annie and Emmitt Kuenzel had both worked at Stevens early in their marriage, but Emmitt rose through the ranks into the management at the mill and Annie found it unnecessary to continue working. Emmitt died suddenly, probably of a heart attack, just before the war, but he left his wife with sufficient resources so that she never needed to return to the mill.

As Mildred and Dave's brood increased to three kids, they began to plan for a home of their own. The Kuenzel home was at the top of the hill, at the back of a two-acre lot in Mt. Lowell, and Mrs. Annie was more than happy to give her daughter and son-in-law enough land for them to build their own home down at the foot of the hill. That way, they would not only be close enough to walk to work but they would be able to help look after her in her declining years. Mildred and Dave got a nothing-down VA loan and built their modest home at the foot of the hill, right beside the gravel drive that snaked up the hill to Mrs. Kuenzel's much bigger house.

Mildred and Dave continued to work as their kids grew into adulthood, and Mrs. Annie, as everyone called her, continued to live alone at the top of the hill. For several years Mildred had been aware that her mother's mental faculties were beginning to slip a bit. Mrs. Annie would forget basic things like whether she had gotten in the mail. Or she might ask Mildred to get her something at the store, when Mildred had gotten it for her just the day before. She still kept her house neat and clean, but she did seem to forget a lot of little things, and Mildred could tell that her mother was awfully lonely.

Sometime early in the 1960's, a guy from Charlotte with a *Royall Tea* franchise began bringing his box van into Mt. Lowell to peddle Royall brand tea and coffee. He also sold spices, patent medicines, cleaning products, and a variety of other stuff. He began to visit Mrs. Kuenzel's home every week.

Mildred and Dave were both working the day shift at the time, so the first Mildred knew about the Royall Tea visits was when she noticed three tins of Royall brand allspice in Mrs. Annie's kitchen cupboard and several bottles of Royall brand patent medicines in the bathroom cabinet. There were also two brand new brooms and two new mops on the back porch. When Mildred questioned her mother about the items, Mrs. Annie professed to know nothing about how those products came to be there. But when she asked the neighbors, they told Mildred that they had been seeing the Royall Tea truck up at Mrs. Kuenzel's house at least one afternoon almost every week.

Mildred never seemed to be able to get home from work early enough to catch the tea salesman at her mother's house, and in the meantime the cans and bottles of Royall Brand oven cleaner, refrigerator deodorizer, headache remedy, and almond extract (not to mention tea) in Mrs. Annie's cupboard continued to grow. It was obvious that Mrs. Annie was lonely, and it was clear that she could no longer remember which home products she already had and which ones she needed. Appar-

ently, all the handsome Royall Tea Man had to do was sit down
with Mrs. Annie for a little chat, complement her a little bit, and
suggest that maybe she needed a little bit of this or a little more
of that. Mrs. Annie always agreed that she needed whatever he
was selling and would end up buying whatever he suggested.
She was not a poor woman, but Mrs. Annie was buying so many
unneeded products that it was beginning to eat into her house-
hold budget.

Mildred was furious. It was not so much about the money spent. But this low-life was sneakily taking advantage of her
mother's condition. Something had to be done. She figured out
that the Royall Tea man had to be visiting her mother on Thurs-
days, so one week she took a half-day of sick leave and came
home early. On this pleasant Thursday afternoon, she sat waiting in the rocking chair on the front porch, perfectly positioned
to stake out the drive that ran across their lot and up the hill her
mother's house. She did not have long to wait for the appearance of the unmistakable Royall Tea van.

The ungainly box van was shaped like a UPS truck, but
it would never be mistaken for one. It was painted red, white and
blue, with a huge image of a sparkling jeweled crown adorning
each side. As it came down the street, it slowed to a crawl, and
then turned up the gravel drive toward Mrs. Annie's house.

Mildred rushed from the porch and stood blocking the
drive, waving the van to a halt. She approached the open door
opposite the driver's side of the van and addressed him in a
most civil manner.

"Sir, are you on your way to visit Mrs. Kuenzel, up on

the hill, there?" She inquired.

"Why, yes ma'am, I am. Not that it is any of your business, but I visit Mrs. Kuenzel most every Thursday."

Mildred was offended by the Tea Man's smart-aleck attitude, but she held her temper. She could see immediately how her mother could be taken in by this sleazy-but-handsome snake oil salesman. She might have been swayed a bit herself, if he hadn't been such a little fellow.

"Well now, Mrs. Kuenzel happens to be my mother, and I consider it my job to look after her best interests. You may not be aware of this," she told him, allowing him the benefit of the doubt, "but Mrs. Kuenzel may be getting a bit senile. She doesn't think too clearly sometimes, and it appears to me that you may be taking advantage of her."

"Oh, she seems just fine to me," the tea man responded. "I only sell her things that she really needs."

"You know sir, Mrs. Kuenzel really does not have a lot of money to spare. I don't think she needs three jars of allspice or three bottles of rheumatism remedy, and I know damn well that she don't need that medicine for menstrual cramps you sold her." Mildred was barely able to keep her voice calm.

The tea man was indignant. "Let me explain something to you ma'am," he intoned, with feigned politeness. "The last time I checked, this is a free country, and that means that I can sell my products to anybody I choose and whenever I wish. It really is none of your business."

Upon hearing that snotty little speech, Mildred just plain lost it. She may have been a large woman, but she was also strong and surprisingly agile. She grabbed the handle beside the van door, and with what appeared to be little effort, she hoisted herself up into the cab with the tea man.

Her face red and her eyes wide with anger, Mildred loomed over the Royall Tea man, who was now quaking behind the wheel of his van. "Well, let me explain something to you, sir," she told him in a loud but even voice, directed right into his face. "I am well aware that this is a free country, and I hope you get rich selling your Royall Tea. But I'll just explain it to you this way. If I ever see your truck going up this hill again, I'll jerk you right out of it and stomp the living shit out of you."

With that, Mildred swung down out of the cab of the truck like a seasoned teamster and stalked back up onto the porch, still steaming.

She stood on her front porch, hands on her hips, glaring at the Royall Tea man, as he hastily backed his van out of the drive and sped down the street. The Royall Tea truck was not seen driving up that hill the following Thursday.

THE PEOPLES' CHOICE

The Democratic Party held sway in North Carolina throughout the 1950's and 1960's to such an extent that winning the Democratic primary for most state-wide offices was the equivalent of being elected. Politics in the state has never been all that exciting when compared to states like Louisiana or Texas, but the 1964 North Carolina Gubernatorial Primary Election was an exception. There were so many candidates, so many incredible characters who had decided that they wanted to serve their state as its governor, that even those citizens who normally displayed little interest in state politics began following this primary election with enthusiasm.

The Democratic front runners were Dan K. Moore, a moderate former superior court judge from Ashville, and a progressive industrialist named Richardson L. Preyer, who happened to be the preferred choice of former governor, Terry Sanford. They both were honorable men, I am sure, and either would have been a competent leader who would have brought honor to the great state of North Carolina. But basics like competence and credentials can seem pretty unexciting when compared to the refreshing persona of candidates from outside the mainstream. That must be why the media across the state pretty much ignored the front runners, probably with the assumption that one of them would win anyway, and concentrated on their more interesting competitors. Listed in order of decreasing viability and increasing entertainment value, the other candidates for the Democratic nomination for governor were as follows.

Number 3, a professor of law from Wake Forest University and a southern gentleman of antebellum tradition, was Dr. I. Beverly Lake. Although he decried racism publicly, it was easy to get the impression that he held a patronizing attitude toward persons of color. Testifying for North Carolina as a friend of the court in 1954, for example, he referred to the Brown vs. Board of Education suit as a "diabolical scheme." He reserved his most outrageous conspiratorial allegations for those he deemed to be communists and subversives, the label he pasted on anyone even slightly to the left of hard-core conservatism. He appeared to believe that nefarious politicians from the left were continually in pursuit of the souls of the folk from all walks of life. He was an early supporter of the infamous North Carolina "speaker-ban law," wherein communists and others deemed to be anti-American were banned from the campuses on North Carolina's state-supported institutions of higher learning.

Number 4, had been recently released after a brief incarceration for alleged involvement in a state contract bid-rigging scheme. Raging against the unreliable business and political associates who had failed to keep him out of jail was former football coach and land developer, Kidd Brewer. As Candidate Brewer drove a road grader sporting white walled tires from town to town in his campaign, he told everyone who would listen that the real culprits in the recent bid-rigging scandal were getting off scot-free. Corruption, he alleged, permeated all the way to the top of the North Carolina political establishment, and it was that establishment, he declared, which had recently sent him up the river as their scapegoat. There may have been some truth to his assertions, but this once powerful force in the North Carolina Democratic Party was now reduced to simply raging against the system.

Number 5, was less well known, but no less entertaining. A banjo-pickin' former deputy sheriff from one of our more rural counties, he was accused of also having once been a moonshiner. Although the precise order of his professions was never made quite clear, at the time of his candidacy he was established as a respectable rural storekeeper. His name was R. J. Stansberry, and the campaign songs he wrote, picked, and sang on North Carolina television provided some of the more humorous aspects of the primary campaign.

Number 6, and the contribution of North Carolina's largest city to the gubernatorial free-for-all, was Bruce "Bozo" Burleson. A former professional wrestler, he was also an engineer who ran on a platform advocating the construction of a monorail connection between Charlotte's Douglas Airport and the (then new) Charlotte Coliseum on Independence Boulevard. He was obviously a man far ahead of his time, and as soon as he realized that the appeal of such a program was limited to folks from the Charlotte area, he proposed similar plans for Greensboro and Raleigh.

To those of us living in Boone, North Carolina, in those days, this primary campaign hubbub seemed remote and surreal. Our television contact with the outside world in those pre-cable days was mostly limited to snowy Winston Salem and Greensboro channels, but if the weather was exceptional, people who lived up a ways on Howard's Knob might also have access to WBTV in Charlotte. The only newspaper available on a regular basis was the Winston Salem Journal, unless you counted the Watauga Democrat, which most people did not.

Radio reception was not much better. Other than late night clear channel station WLAC Nashville, Tennessee, the only reliable station available was Boone's own WATA. This 200-watt marvel of modern communications covered the southern skies from Sugar Grove to Deep Gap and from Blowing Rock to Tater Hill. Morning programming on WATA mostly consisted of what was then called hillbilly music, with occasional relief provided by local and headline news. Listeners were also frequently treated to sermons by local wind-sucking preachers, and twice daily they could hear "The Obituary Column of the Air." It is rumored that the station apologized to its listeners for canceling this program one morning when, in the announcers own words, "We are very sorry, but there are no obituaries today."

Morning programming on WATA was so bad during the week that when the Ole Farm and Home Pro-gram came on at noon, the number of people tuned in to the station actually increased. The morning country music/preaching format ran six days a week, but at noon on Saturday "Farm and Home" was replaced by a local program called Lets All Go Down Town. This radio program was conducted in a "man on the street" interviewer format, and was sponsored by the Boone Merchants Association. The program was pretty much of a Chamber of Commerce infomercial, designed to entice the local area folks into town to shop. It was broadcast live from downtown Boone, downtown Boone being right outside the door of the radio station. This provided the advantage of requiring minimal remote broadcast equipment for the production of the program, along with a very long microphone cable.

"Let's All Go Downtown" programming consisted of frequent interviews with the local merchants regarding their unbelievable sales on fine merchandise, punctuated by promotions of upcoming sports events at the college, and spontaneous interviews with pedestrians who happened by. Area residents who had come into downtown Boone to loaf, get something from the hardware store, or maybe get a haircut, were typically interviewed.

Usually, there would also be some live music performed by a local group. One group whose music I recall as being especially enjoyable was a Western Swing Trio called "The String A-Longs." This group was notable primarily because of the virtuosity of the electric guitar player, a fellow whom I believe went by the name of Arthel Watson back then. In the broadcasts conducted during the fall season, typical person-on-the street interview questions ran along the lines of "Think we are in for a rough winter this year?" a question replaced with "Well, do you think winter is about over?" queries in the spring. (If you had lived in Boone in the 1960's, you would understand why winter weather was a topic of such intense interest.)

On one bright Saturday afternoon in October, downtown Boone was exceptionally crowded, a large number of flatland leaf gazers having traveled to the mountains and mingled with the local throng. It was just a few days before the primary, so naturally, that was the topic the interviewer wanted to discuss with the folks on the street. He had accosted a gentleman on the sidewalk on this particular afternoon, taking him by the arm and thrusting the microphone into his face. After establishing that he was from Vilas, North Carolina, the announcer asked the gentleman whom he thought would be chosen as the Democratic candidate for governor of the State of North Carolina.

"Waaal..." the interviewee allowed, it's "kind'a hard for me to say."

As the announcer pursued his questioning, the radio listeners could actually hear the fellow scratching the stubble on his chin as he pondered the questions.

"Don't get no tellyvision up whar I live." He continued. "Muh radio's broke. And 'atair Watauga Demmycrat really ain't hardly worth readin'." He then paused and gazed out into the street.

"But while I been standin' here, I been a-countin' the bumper stickers on these here cars a-goin' up and down the street." Again he paused thoughtfully.

"And it 'pears to me like **R. R. Tweetsie** has got this here election in a landslide."

RELIGION 101*

To tell the truth, I never worked too hard in school. And neither did my friend, Benny Creed. Benny and me were assigned to be roommates when we first got here as freshmen in 1959, and we got along so well that we roomed together for our first two years and we remained close friends for all four.

We were both Business Education majors, not exactly a tough course of study, and we went through that whole program at Appalachian together. That's how we got to be roommates in the first place, and we were usually able to register for the same classes. We were in the same classes most of the time we were in school.

Since neither one of us studied too hard, there was almost never a conflict where one of us wanted to study and the other one didn't. If one of us wanted to have a poker game in the room some night, and the other one had a test the next day, that was no problem. We would both just end up playing poker. That is just an example of why we got along so well.

Winter quarter of the senior year, all seniors received their notice that they need to come by the registrar's office for a graduation check. The checks showed that Benny and I were each just one course short in the humanities requirement and that we were both just slightly below the 2.0 grade point average required for graduation. This meant that if I was going to graduate in May, I had to find an easy humanities course to take spring quarter and that I also had to make a B grade or better in everything I was taking. Anything less and I would have to attend summer school, maybe both sessions, before I could graduate. All that applied to Benny as well.

We read the course catalog and asked around, trying to find a really crib humanities course that would fit our needs. We did find plenty of interesting humanities courses, but some of them sounded awfully tough. There was *Russian Literature and Culture,* which sounded really tough, there was *Greek Mythology,* which sounded kind of tough, and then there was *The Fairy Tale as Literature*, which seemed like a real possibility. Lucky for us, a friend had once registered for that course, and he warned us not to be fooled. In fact, the course was so hard, he dropped it after two weeks. "Can you imagine having to read a bunch of fairytales, searching for a hidden meaning and analyzing the philosophies expressed in them?" he lamented. But our friend did have a recommendation for a better choice that would fulfill our humanities requirement. It was *REL 101: Western Religions*.

We were told that the same professor had taught that course every spring quarter for many, many years. The course was taught by an ancient emeritus professor, Dr. Caruthers, who was also a retired minister. Most important though, he was a really easy grader. It was reported that he would just wander into the class room and read from his ancient yellowed notes for about fifty minutes, and then leave, usually without bothering to even call roll. He gave the same three multiple-choices quizzes every time he taught the course. He dutifully returned all test papers to the students after grading them, so copies of his old quizzes were easy to find. He even gave the same final exam at the end of the course, year after year. Our friend, who recommended the class, just happened to still have his copies of all of the old quizzes and the final exam. Home free!

Dr. Caruthers let everyone know on the first day of class that his definition of "Western Religion" was basically a review of Protestant Christianity as revealed through the King James Bible. Benny and I didn't have any problems with that. We went straight to the library and checked out a KJB, just in case we needed a reference.

We did not work too hard for Professor Caruthers, needless to say. It took all of our time to keep the grades up in our other classes. We usually only went to Western Religions on quiz days, and since we had copies of the tests before hand, we did okay on most of them. We never used crib sheets, though. We may have been lazy students, but we were not cheaters.

Coming into the final, though, we both figured that we had just about C+ averages in REL 101. This meant that we both had to get at least a B+ on the final exam to bring our term average up to the required B and get our grade point average up to the required 2.0. Otherwise, it would be summer school for us. The pressure was on.

We were still confident, though. We had advance detailed knowledge of Professor Caruthers's final exam. For years, the final had consisted of just one essay question, always the same one: "Trace the travels of the Apostle Paul." Writing out our examination essay out in advance, though, would have been considered cheating. Besides, in those days, all examinations had to be written into the exam bluebooks which were handed out to the students by the professor just before the exam.

The evening before the Western Religions final, we spent most of the night tracing the travels of the Apostle Paul. The next morning, as we confidently walked into the REL 101 classroom and took our seats, we both felt sure that we were going to ace the exam.

Dr. Caruthers soon came doddering into the room and passed out the blue books. He then walked to the front of the room and wrote the examination on the board: "REL 101, Final Examination: Write a critical analysis of the moral teachings revealed through the Sermon on the Mount."

I was staggered! Although I could recall from the Sunday school classes I attended as a kid that there was something called "The Sermon on the Mount," at that moment and under such pressure, I couldn't remember a thing about it. The only thing I was the least bit prepared for was tracing the travels of the Apostle Paul.

There was nothing I could do. My mind was blank and I was completely stumped. I wrote a short note on the inside cover of my blue book explaining to the professor that I was suffering from a severe attack of test anxiety that morning and was therefore unable to complete the exam. Then I just signed my name and turned in my bluebook with all of the pages blank. As I was leaving, though, I could not help but notice that my friend Benny was humped over his desk, writing away, just as though he knew exactly what he was doing. I thought that seemed very strange.

Needless to say, I received an F in the course. It would be summer school for me, and it would probably take both sessions to both complete my humanities requirement and get my grade point average back up to the level required for graduation. As I was sadly packing up to go home for the break, Benny strolled into the room, whistling merrily. "Well, we sure blew that religion course," I told him.

"What do you mean 'we'?" he countered. "I got B+ in the course and a big A on the examination."

"Now, how the dickens could that happen?" I demanded to know. "We studied together, and what's more important, we avoided studying together. What could you possibly know about the Sermon on the Mount that I didn't know?"

"Well, I just went by Dr. Caruther's office to check on my grade and he gave me my exam book back. Want to see how I did?" Benny handed me his exam bluebook. The first thing I noticed was the big red "A" scrawled on the cover.

I opened Benny's bluebook and began to read. Here is the word according to Benny: *Let those who will criticize the words of the Master. As for me, I shall trace the travels of the Apostle Paul.*

*Note: One of my professors told this story to our class. He said that the story was told to him by the late North Carolina Governor Terry Sanford, who described it as one of his favorites.

If you have studied long and hard, then you should be able to tell when someone is talking rot, and that is the major benefit of an education.

— Harold Wilson

THE POWER OF MUSIC

There were no Pell grants and few low-interest loans available for students in the early 1960's. Even with help from the National Science foundation, students such as I usually found it necessary to take on part time jobs in order to continue with our educations. Of course, keeping a job usually requires access to a reliable automobile. But then, owning and maintaining a car requires additional income. This is often the beginning of a vicious cycle that can continue for years, possibly even for a lifetime.

I definitely had to have a car. After a lengthy and agonizing process, I settled on the purchase of an almost new Volkswagen Beetle, a vehicle which had not been available in the United States for all that long. The car was becoming popular with young folks, hippies, college students, and the like, but it was considered by conservative gear heads to be the antithesis of what a "real" automobile should be. The story about the fundamentalist radio preacher who railed against the Volkswagen, declaring that "If the Lord had meant for a car to have its engine in the rear, he would have put the hood ornament on the trunk!" was probably just a joke, however.

My dad, a pretty knowledgeable mechanic, had serious misgivings about my purchase of any foreign car, but especially one with the engine in the rear. He warned me, correctly as it turned out, that the extra weight in the rear of the car, combined with a swing-axle rear suspension, was likely to cause the car to be unstable if required to execute an extreme emergency maneuver. (Why Ralph Nader decided to attack the Corvair rather than the much-less-stable VW Beetle has long been a mystery to me. It probably can best be understood if one is aware that Nader had not yet obtained his driver's license at the time he wrote his infamous book, *Unsafe at Any Speed.*)

In many ways, the VW was probably as good a choice as I could have made. It was reliable, inexpensive to buy, and economical to operate. But above all, girls thought it was cute. For a guy who can only afford a car which is neither sporty nor prestigious, the best he can hope for is *cute*.

The 1960's sixties folk music craze was just beginning about this time, and since little real talent was required for someone to declare themselves to be a folk singer, I became one. A couple of nights a week I was able to earn a few extra bucks playing and singing "The Music of the People" in a Durham night spot. The regulars there were an odd mixture of button-down business and law students from Duke, glassy-eyed hippie sociology majors from UNC, and a motley collection of drop-outs and hangers-on. It was exactly the clientele one would expect to find in a joint located in a basement near a university campus and bearing a name such as *The Null and Void*. This so-called coffee house sold much more beer than coffee, and many of the clientele also smoked strange-smelling cigarettes.

It was the summer of 1962, when another folksinger and I were playing alternating sets, two nights a week, from about nine o'clock until midnight in this establishment. The place always shut down soon after midnight, that being the hour at which the sale of alcohol became verboten in Durham County, North Carolina. (They could have continued to sell coffee, however, should anyone have ordered any.)

Shortly after midnight on one such night, I packed up my guitar and began loading up my car. One of the downsides of the Beetle was its limited luggage capacity, but I had my packing developed into a fine art. My acoustic guitar fit precisely into the up-front trunk of the VW, while the well-worn vintage sound system, my banjo, and my tenor guitar could all be snugly jammed into the lowered back seat. (The right front seat was always kept in reserve, just in case I got lucky some night.) Most nights, by half-past midnight I was all loaded up and headed down the highway to my little garage apartment a few miles north of Fayetteville. That was the place that I was then calling home because it was cheap and sort of convenient to both my day job and to school.

This particular night, I was cruising a bit too fast down NC Highway 55, somewhere just south of Holly Springs, when a sudden thumping from the right rear of the car accompanied by a frightful lurching of the suddenly unstable vehicle informed me that a rear tire had blown out. After a terrifying few seconds of frantically sawing on the steering wheel, as the car swung back and forth across the road, I somehow regained control. As I slowed to a shaky crawl along the shoulder, I could see a cluster of buildings and a parking lot on the left just ahead. All of the businesses in the cluster appeared to be closed, but a section of the parking lot in front was lighted. It looked like the best location for changing a tire that I was likely to find around there. I bumped into the lot and brought the car to a stop near the center of a circle of light cast by a flood light mounted high above the front door of the Fuquay-Varina Feed and Seed Store.

I opened up the front trunk of the VW and, after a brief search, located and extracted the jack and the combined lug wrench/jack handle. The tools were immaculate, so I figured this must be the first time they had ever been used. A quick examination of the jack revealed simple, straight-forward design, leaving no great mechanical mysteries to be solved.

At some point in my life I had been told that the recommended procedure when changing a tire on any car was to break all of the lug nuts loose on the offending wheel before jacking it up. This I accomplished after a minor struggle which included fitting the lug wrench on the lug nut, then stomping the jack handle and chanting appropriate profanities until the nut broke free. Eventually, I succeeded in freeing all four lug nuts and rotating them the recommended initial half-turn. Then I began jacking up the car.

I had inserted the jack into the socket in the quarter panel in front of the flat tire (early Volkswagen Beetles had built-in jack sockets) and was jacking up the car, when I thought I was hearing music. A moment later I knew that I did indeed hear music, someone was playing a piano and someone was singing! As I looked up and over the rear of the car, two people staggered out through a patch of light glowing from a door near the back of a ramshackle old wooden structure located far at the other end of the parking lot. When the door closed behind the people passing through it, the sound of the piano was snuffed out, but the singing continued.

The two who had emerged from the door disappeared into the darkness, but I could tell from the singing that they were moving my way. Then two disheveled characters of comically contrasting appearance lurched from the darkness into the circle of light in front of the feed store. I guessed that the building down the lot was an illegal juke joint and that these were two of its patrons on their way home.

I quickly recognized the song they were singing as a mildly lewd beach music song made popular a few years earlier by *The Midnighters*, one of a series of songs that Hank Ballard wrote and sang about a woman of dubious reputation named Annie.

"You gotta work with me Annie," sang the tall, lanky one in a pretty good baritone.

"All right baby," the short, chubby one squeaked in a cracked falsetto.

"You gotta work with me baby," rumbled the baritone.

"Don't mean maybe," quavered the chubby one.

My initial apprehension quickly disappeared as I realized that these two were aware of nothing in the world outside of their singing and the quart bottle of Black Label Beer that each of them carried by the neck. They alternated drinking and singing; every other line, one would grab a swig of beer as the other sang a part, and vice versa.

"You gotta work with me Annie." Swig.

"All right baby." Chug. "Belch."

As they meandered across the circle of light, the tall one

abruptly stopped by the front of my car, his bottle poised in front of his open mouth and his head tilted to the side, as he peered into the open trunk of the VW. He then scratched his head and called out, "Hey Joe!" in a hoarse whisper.

Joe continued to putter on, unaware that his companion had fallen behind. "Work with me A-an-nie. All right! You gotta get it while the getting' is good, so good , so good." Chubby Joe was now singing both parts to the song.

"Joe. Hey Joe." The baritone guy was now calling louder, more urgently. "Hey Joe! Man, you gotta see this." He was animatedly pointing into the open trunk in the front of the Beetle.

At last Joe turned around and weaved back toward to his compatriot, continuing to swig and sing all the while. "Work with me A-a-nee...urp."

"Joe! Look here," the tall one continued to insist.

Joe finally staggered up to the side of his friend and supported himself by reaching up and grabbing his friend's shoulder and hanging on.

"Man, would you look at that?" The tall one instructed his wobbly companion, as he gestured toward the open front of the car with his beer bottle.

"Do you see that, Joe? Look right there. This here car is powered by a git-tar!"

PANDORA'S PRIDE

The Educational Psychology class we were all required to take at Appalachian State was really not all that demanding. Still, some of Professor Fracker's lectures about working with secondary school students included principles that all aspiring teachers should have taken to heart. Some of the things we were told in his class I can still remember after fifty years. Many of them seem obvious to me now, but they were useful revelations at the time.

"You can't make all of the students like you, but that should not be your main objective anyway. Your students really don't have to like you as a friend to understand that you have their best interest at heart."

"It is just as important for the students to feel that they are respected by the teacher as it is for the teacher to feel respected by the students."

"Young junior high and high school students, can be really sensitive about some seemingly insignificant things. This is a very fragile age, an age when many young people go through periods of self-loathing – at times they dislike everything about themselves – their appearance, their parents, even their own names."

"A teacher should never comment on a student's name, no matter how matter interesting or unusual," he told us. "Even just a benign comment, sometimes even a compliment, can be taken in completely the wrong way. Try to act as though every student's name is as common

as John Smith. And if you do happen to have
a student named John Smith, please do not ask
him about Pocahontas."

"If a student's name brings to mind a humorous association or a pun, the teacher should
absolutely avoid any reference to it. Chances
are, students with unusual names have already
been kidded about their names by their schoolmates throughout their elementary school years.
They certainly don't need to hear it from their
teachers. Make every effort to avoid displaying
the slightest hint of amusement over a student's
name."

Looking back, I also have to wonder if Professor Fracker ever had an international student with a name like Long Du-
ong, or a flirtatious wild-thing with a name like Pandora Picklesimer in any of his classes. Long understood what the joke
was with his name and he really did not seem to care. But guys
in classes with Ms. Picklesimer were continually making jokes
about the poor girl's name, usually by making some snickering
allusion to Pandora's Box. About all I could do was to pretend
that I didn't hear them. Through my long career as an educator,
I have collected a list of students' names which would make any
teacher reluctant to even call roll.

About three fourths of the high school students in the
small town where I began my teaching career appeared to have
no plans to ever live anywhere else. I think the students there
had just as much innate ability as any group of students I ever
encountered, but the motivation was definitely lacking. There

were a few students who had plans to go to college after high school, while some others went into military service. The fact is, though, most of the young people who left that town after high school never returned. Many of the students saw their future as simply one of working in the local factories from the day they graduated until they either retired or died. High school was the place where one might happen to learn a little something (probably not very useful, most thought) while playing sports, leading cheers, or just socializing. But first and foremost, high school was the place where one would meet and woo his or her future mate.

Disinterested students typically do not enroll in trigonometry and physics classes, and most of the students I had in those classes were well motivated to learn. But since I got to teach those advanced students, my course assignment had to be balanced out with some of the lower level classes such as General Math and Algebra I. Pandora Picklesimer was in my Algebra I class.

Pandora was such a strikingly beautiful young woman, if she had ever absorbed one smidgen of sophistication, there is no telling what she could have done in life. We probably would have been seeing her on stage and screen. But she was pure mill town, from the soles of her cute little Keds to the bow on her bounteous blonde bouffant.

One of the school counselors told me that the girl had blossomed into voluptuous womanhood at an age of about twelve. Two years later and in my algebra class, it was clear that she still did not quite know what to make of it all. So far as

I could tell, she had only three things on her mind: older boys, boys her age, and one boy in particular. I think she ended up in my Algebra I instead of General Math because the boy who was currently on her radar was also in that class. But just because she liked one boy especially did not mean that she could not flirt with every other guy on the planet. Whatever her motivations, she definitely did not sign up for the class because she wanted to learn algebra.

For someone who never did any math homework and did not try very hard on the quizzes, Miss Picklesimer's grades were not quite as bad as she probably deserved. They were just good enough to convince me that she could do quite well, if she would make even a little bit of effort. But her terrible attitude was demoralizing to the whole class. Having a student in class who is disinterested in math is one thing, but having one who continually, loudly, vocalizes about how this class (and high school in general) is wasting her valuable time is much more problematic. Pandora would tell other students at every oppor-tunity, "This place is the pits! Next year when I'm sixteen, it's going to be adios, amigos, and I'm gonna' be outa here!"

Of course, there was always the possibility that Pandora was just deliberately doing poorly in the class because the boy she had taken a shine to was also not doing too well. But at least he appeared to be trying. He had to study to stay eligible to play football, and he had even told me that he was hopeful that he might be offered a college scholarship. I tried to convince Pandora that if she would learn a little more algebra, maybe she could tutor the boy she liked and improve both of their math performances, but she saw right through my amateurish attempt to use psychology. She was not interested in math and the both of them continued to flounder.

Denny Joyce, head of the math and science program at the school, was a man with years of experience teaching math and someone with a reputation as an excellent teacher. I asked him if he had any ideas about how Pandora might be motivated into learning some math. But at the mention of Pandora's name, Mr. Joyce just kind of laughed and asked, "What is your problem with Pandora?"

When I explained Pandora's disruptive behavior, he rolled out the latest educational fad by asking, "Have you considered that Pandora's behavior might be because of her low self-esteem?"

Now, it had occurred to me that Pandora might suffer from certain minor personality defects, but low self-esteem was not one which had ever come to mind. In fact, I had judged that Pandora might have had a bit of an excessively high opinion of herself. But I understood Mr. Joyce's diagnosis a little better when he told me that other students had picked on her and called her "pickle" during her elementary school years.

That was not the first time I had heard low self-esteem suggested as a reason for poor academic performance, and I was going to hear a lot more about it in the future. For several years "enhancing the students' self-esteem" was the educational fad promoted as the sure-fire way to improve student performance. Several times in the seventies, I had a student bring a paper with a truly terrible grade up to me and insist, "This grade can't be right. Everybody tells me that I'm such a good student."

In Miss Picklesimer's case, Mr. Joyce suggested that, since she so enjoyed being the center of attention, perhaps I should ask her more questions in class. That would focus more of her classmates attention on her, and she would probably not want to appear dumb. Furthermore, he suggested, since student self-esteem was such a critical factor affecting student performance, I should take care to compliment and encourage her on her performance in math, whether it was deserved or not.

Well, although I doubted that Pandora Picklesimer suffered from any low level of self-esteem, I decided that his suggestions were worth trying.

The next day in the algebra class, I singled out Pandora for the answer to a simple algebra question. She responded with rolling eyes, a dismissive shrug, and a classic "I dunno. I can't do this algebra stuff."

Then I directed the question to another student, but when he was unable to answer, I decided to give Pandora a second chance. Since it was an especially easy problem, I walked over and stood near Pandora's desk so I could at least see if she was attempting to solve it. She did make a few scribbles on her paper and I thought maybe she had at least gotten an answer.

"What did you get for the average speed in this problem, Miss Picklesimer?" I asked.

"You better ask somebody else, Mr. Mack," she responded. "I ain't got no idear."

"Aw, come now Miss Picklesimer," I pursued. "You're a pretty good math student. What did you get?"

"I didn't get no answer, Mr. Mack," she grumped. "I just couldn't do it."

I should have gone on to another student right then, but I continued to bug Pandora. "I thought I saw you solve this problem, Pandora. I saw you working on it. Tell me what you got for an answer."

Pandora had been pushed too far. "Mr. Mack," she loudly complained, "You know I ain't no good in math."

Then just in case anyone in the class was unaware of her true feelings, she jumped to her feet and placed her hands defiantly on her hips. Then, twisting around to face the class, she threw her head back and delivered her Jeremiad. "I ain't no dang good in algebra, Mr. Mack, and you know it. **I ain't one bit smart neither... and I'm proud uv it!**"

When I think back
On all the crap I learned in high school
It's a wonder
I can think at all.
But my lack of education
Hasn't hurt me none.
I can read the writing on the wall.
　　　　—Paul Simon, *Kodachrome*

No Amount of Careful Planning

Even as I completed my program, I could feel Uncle Sam breathing heavily down my neck. I was attending the University of North Carolina compliments of the *National Defense Education Act,* and as they say, if the government giveth, the government can taketh away. Had I thought that our country was truly facing a clear and present danger, however, I would not have been quite so fixated on the draft.

As it turned out, the government had other plans for me anyway, and they were a way down south in Texas. There was to be a stint at Texas A&M learning new and exciting things, followed by work in a project at a university research facility in a remote region of Southwest Texas. The job was classified as a critical occupation, which also meant a guaranteed draft deferment. Almost immediately I felt that I may have made a mistake in accepting it.

There's no need to spend time complaining, other than to declare that the location of the facility was as remote and as dry as the far side of the moon and that the work was hot, tedious, and hazardous. I also thought that the long term effect of the project could be environmentally devastating. It was actually a great sense of relief when, after just a few months on the job, I learned that the government was cancelling the project. The reasons given for the cancellation were mostly economic, citing a need for the money to be used in other projects. I also had a feeling that some wise person way up the ladder saw the project in much the same way I did.

Some of the higher-level personnel were offered opportunities to transfer to other projects, but most of the newbies like me were simply canned. We were given a personal liability waver and a non-disclosure agreement to sign, two week's severance pay, and bidden a fond farewell. In the middle of November, I found myself leaving West Texas headed for Chapel Hill, North Carolina, hoping to get back into graduate school for spring semester.

Anyone who doesn't know that it's a long way across Texas should take the scenic drive from Odessa to Longview sometime. At least Texas is not so hot in November, and just watching Longview disappear in my rear-view mirror as I neared Louisiana made it all worth the trip. If there is not a country song that says something like that, there should be.

Although my original destination was Chapel Hill, as I headed up from Atlanta, it occurred to me that the day was the Wednesday before Thanksgiving, and by the time I got there, the administrative offices would be closed. There was nothing that could be accomplished by my getting to Chapel Hill any time before the next Monday. But I did have friends in Charlotte who had put me up before, and they might be willing to do it again. Charlotte was on my original route anyway, and since it was just a few hours away, it became my new destination.

My friends did seem genuinely glad to see me, and they said they would be willing to let me stay with them for a few days, provided I brought my guitar. I had it with me, but it had not been out of the case for six months. It took a couple of days to catch up on old times, who was where, recently married and or divorced, and who now had how many kids. We didn't get around to playing music until Friday night, at which time I discovered that I was pitifully out of practice and the strings on my guitar were totally dead.

Saturday morning found me at Tillman's Music Store on Independence Boulevard in Charlotte, looking for new guitar strings. I had shopped at Tillman's before, and I planned to look for some new music while I was there. "I had better learn some new tunes," I thought. "I might have to go back to playing for food."

The first thing I noticed when I entered the store was that there was a very pretty lady working behind the counter. She was occupied with a customer at the time, so I browsed around for a while. I found a new Gordon Lightfoot songbook (he was big at the time) and a little book of Pete Seeger's Sing Out Reprints. The instrument strings, however, were kept behind the counter. As I approached the counter a second time, the pretty lady was talking on the phone, but just a minute later she put the phone down and looked up at me. At that moment I found myself looking into the most gorgeous pair of brown eyes I had ever seen.

"How may I help you?" I think that was what she said to me. I had trouble finding my voice to answer. I finally asked if they had a book of John Prine songs – something, anything, that would give me a chance to talk to her. She came out from behind the counter and efficiently led me to precisely what I had asked about. The search took far less time than I had hoped.

When we returned to the counter I desperately wanted

an excuse to talk to her. I honestly did think that I had seen her someplace before, so of course I had to ask, "Don't I know you from somewhere?" She just frowned a little and rolled her gorgeous eyes as if to say "How many times have I heard that one?" She was sure that she didn't know me from anywhere.

Luckily, there were no other customers waiting, and she seemed willing enough to chat with me for a little while. I learned that, unlike most of the people who worked there, she was not a serious musician. This discovery made me suspect that Tillman's just hired her to attract customers like me. When I asked if she could go out with me that weekend, of course she told me she was going to be too busy. And that, I assumed, was going to be that.

On Sunday a friend pointed out a job listing in the Charlotte Observer for a physics instructor at Central Piedmont Community College The opening was for a teaching position beginning winter quarter, beginning in just a few days. I wasn't actually looking for a job, but I did have some worries about getting back into school for spring semester. My chances for the next fall were much better, but I didn't have a big reserve of funds, and by next fall I could be drafted. Maybe I should take a teaching job for a while.

Until that day, I had never even heard of the college, but my friends assured me that it was a rapidly growing and well respected institution. The wave of the future, I believe they called it. The job at Central Piedmont Community College sounded like something I should check into.

Early Monday morning I called the school and was invited to come to the college for an immediate interview. I soon found my way to the Administration Building on Elizabeth Avenue, and as soon as the executive vice president was informed by his secretary that they had an applicant for the physics teaching job, things moved forward rather quickly. After a cursory interview (just enough questions to make sure that I was not wasting their time), I was given a quick tour of the college, handed an application form, and asked to fill it out right then. They said the transcripts and recommendations could be handled later.

As I sat in the lobby outside of the Vice President's Office filling out the application, I was struggling with uncertainties, such as recalling the official address of the last place I worked and whom to list as my references.   Then, as I was wondering how precise I needed to be in listing my previous salary, I heard a somewhat familiar voice saying, "Well…, don't I know you from somewhere?"

I looked up from the application to again be mesmerized by those same eyes I had encountered in the music store just two days before. "You talkin' to me?"

It seems that the lovely lady who worked at Tillman's on Saturdays was someone who also took classes and worked part-time at the community college. How many times in life does one get such a second chance? "After I finish filling out this application," I suggested, "why don't we have lunch together? I hear that Jimmy's Restaurant across the street is pretty good." She graciously accepted my invitation, even though she probably guessed that I had not known there was a Jimmy's

Restaurant until about an hour before. I just happened to park near it on my way to apply for the job.

To say that our impromptu luncheon date went well would be an understatement. As it turned out, I really may have known her from somewhere else. At another school, years before and far away, she had lived in the same dormitory as a girl I was dating at that time. The fact that the girl I had been dating then was someone whom this young lady did not particularly like appeared to not hurt my case at all.

We lingered in Jimmy's long after we finished our meal, and it seemed to me that something special happened during that time. We had been in the restaurant over two hours when she looked at her watch and exclaimed, "Oh, my God! I just missed my history class."

The short version of the story is this: I did get the job at Central Piedmont Community College, I did not get drafted, and the lovely lady whom I met in the music store and I have been married for over forty years. Not a bad outcome for stopping off for a long weekend on my way to someplace else. Like they say, no amount of careful planning will ever replace dumb luck.

"You got to be careful if you don't know where you're going, because you might not get there."
— Yogi Berra

I'd Just as Soon Be in Boone

Sergeant Lester Harrison Powers participated in most of the Allies' European campaign of the Second World War. He served with distinction in the United States Army, first in Italy, then across France and into Germany. Les Powers then spent much of the remainder of his life extolling the proposition that anyone who had not served in the military was not truly educated. Perhaps he was right – it was his military service that made it possible for him to attend North Carolina State University under the G.I. Bill and earn his degree in mechanical engineering.

Years later, as the Department Chairman of the Engineering Technology Program at *Peneplain Community College*, he continually sang the praises of the Servicemen's Readjustment Act, (usually simply referred to as the G.I. Bill). He would go out of his way to assist any veteran who might have an interest in enrolling at PPCC, especially for someone interested in the Engineering Technology Program. But even fifty years after the end of WWII, it was easy to tell that Les Powers's psyche had not emerged from the two years of heavy combat duty unscathed.

In spite of a strong sense of fairness on racial issues and a welcoming attitude toward most of the international students enrolled at the college, L. H. Powers harbored a deep seated suspicion of the descendants of his old World War II enemies until the end of his life. One manifestation of this attitude was his open hostility towards products of foreign manufacture, especially German automobiles.

"Those bastards tried to kill me," Les would announce to anyone whom he knew to have purchased a Volkswagen or a Mercedes. "I can't see how any patriotic American could ever consider buying one of their Goddamned cars!" If someone he knew bought a foreign car, he might even offer them the opinion that he considered the purchase of a Japanese or German automobile to be an act bordering on treason. For years he refused to ride in my old imported Diesel, declaring that it sounded like a truck and smelled like a kerosene stove, but I did not take it personally.

Like so many truly awful drivers, he considered himself to be the only capable driver on the road, and he detested riding in a car driven by anyone else. That was only one item on a very long list of things that he truly detested, including his own name. L. H. Powers would tolerate no one other than his wife ever calling him *Lester,* and he would grumble if ever a colleague called him *Les,* rather than the more professional, and therefore to be preferred, *L.H.*

Lester Harrison Powers, P.E. (Professional Engineer) eventually moved up to a position as the Director of the Engineering Technology Program at Peneplain Community College. He then immediately began to apply all of his military values to departmental policies. Perhaps it was not too unreasonable for him to require all of the instructors in his department to wear neckties every day and to always call him *Mr. Powers.* However, his demands that his faculty never chew gum, never use toothpicks, and never whistle or hum, even unconsciously, in his presence, put him dangerously close to the nutcase category. I considered myself fortunate that he was only my colleague and friend, and not my boss. A friend of mine from the chemistry department earned the undying enmity of L.H., when as a joke, he walked into Les's office, simultaneously chewing gum and whistling, with a toothpick dangling from the corner of his mouth. It was an admittedly childish thing to do – it required hours of practice in advance – but it really did not merit the threats of physical violence it produced.

One of Mr. Power's favorite homilies was, "The more things change, they more they stay the same." Well, that was definitely true for him. Like some other professional engineers of modest ability whom I have known, he despised change. But L. H. Powers carried his own resistance to change to a new level. When electronic calculators first came out in the early1970's, he – as well as some other instructors in the engineering, mathematics, and accounting programs – refused to allow students to use them in class. In the early days of calculators, when they cost a couple of hundred dollars, the claim that allowing their use in taking tests was unfair to the students who could not afford them was probably valid. But as the cost of calculators plummeted, more and more instructors relented and allowed their use. But Les never adapted and continued to insist that he could see no advantage in their use. Near the end of his life, he would actually boast to his colleagues that he had never, not even once, used an electronic calculator.

It was this unreasonable resistance to change that put an end to his career. His profane reaction when the vice president over his department suggested that perhaps it was time for the Engineering Technology Department to begin teaching classes in computer assisted drafting (commonly known as CAD) convinced his boss that the Engineering Technology Department needed a change in leadership. Fortunately, L.H. Powers could afford to retire anyway.

The man was an amazing compound of contradictions. One did not have to converse with L.H. Powers very long to learn that he held some pretty liberal political and religious views, all the while remaining a champion of Victorian sexual mores and continuing to insist that the proper place for a woman was in the home. L. H. Powers was known to be severely tight-fisted with his personal and family finances, but he was capable of acts of amazing generosity toward people he believed to be genuinely in need.

One of his many acts of generosity was his long-term funding of a nephew's college education. Les had several sisters, one of whom was widowed at a fairly young age and left with two young children and limited resources. Les and one of the sisters agreed that they would somehow provide for the children's college educations, Les providing for the education of the nephew and his sister for the niece. Les and his sister naturally assumed that the children would attend one of the affordable North Carolina state colleges or universities.

When the nephew reached college age, Les willingly accepted the financial responsibility for his higher education. As a graduate engineer from North Carolina State University, however, L. H. Powers not only insisted that the nephew attend that institution, but that he choose engineering as his major. The nephew did have a decent high school record, and his uncle thought that he should major in a field which would insure him a good paying job.

Upon graduation from high school, the nephew did enroll in the School of Engineering at N.C. State, in keeping with his uncle's wishes. The initial results, unfortunately, were not so good. The nephew did not like the engineering program at State, and the engineering program did not like him. In fact, about the only things he liked about the university were the many parties organized by the fraternity he had joined. The family was dismayed by his mediocre academic performance, but the nephew was not sufficiently embarrassed to buckle down and become a serious student.

After a disastrous first year at N. C. State, the nephew declared his intention to transfer to Appalachian State University, a school with a slightly lower academic status at that time, and no engineering program. After a lot of bluster and threats to cut off the nephew's support, Uncle L.H. relented and agreed to fund a year at ASU. Then they would see how things might go from there.

At Appalachian State the nephew began a series of experimentations with various majors while continuing to expand his social life. Chemistry with an eye toward pre-med was the major for his first disastrous year at ASU, followed by an equally disastrous year in accounting. At the end of each of those years, although Les Powers would threaten to terminate his support, the nephew would display the required degree of contrition, and the uncle would always relent. Lester had made a sacred promise to his sister, and one thing about L. H. Powers – a promise made was a promise kept.

In his fourth year of college, the nephew settled into a psychology major, a program which allowed him to both maintain his rich social life and make decent grades. The original timetable for the nephew's university education had him graduating in four years, possibly five, had he majored in engineering. At ASU, however, the nephew's college experience extended into a sixth and eventually, into a seventh year.

In fairness to the nephew, it should be noted he did take on part-time jobs to help defray some of the expenses for the last few years he was in school. He worked as a grounds-keeper for a time and he later maintained an extensive tenure as a pizza delivery man. He even worked as an ersatz Indian, attacking the train at Tweetsie Rail Road one summer. All of these were meaningful life experiences to be sure, and in this process, the nephew created many friendships and developed a considerable fondness for the wonderful mountain university town of Boone, North Carolina.

At last, after fourteen regular semesters and countless summer sessions, the nephew was cleared to graduate. Les escorted a large family contingent to Boone for the graduation festivities, and following the ceremony, Les treated the entire family to a celebratory dinner in a nice Boone restaurant. Naturally, the conversation over dinner eventually turned to the nephew's plans for the future.

"Have you any prospects for a job?" Les wanted to

know, worried that the employment prospects for someone with the nephew's erratic academic record might not be all that great.

"Well, I have had a few nibbles," the nephew waffled. "I applied to an insurance company in Raleigh, but I haven't heard anything from them. And I am thinking about applying for a job at the new BMW plant in South Carolina. I have heard that they have a need for personnel managers."

"Do you have interviews scheduled with any of these folks?" the uncle pointedly pursued his questioning.

"Well, no," the Nephew admitted. "I really haven't talked to anyone yet. Actually, I am hoping to stay here in Boone. I would really like to live in Boone."

After his seven year investment in his nephew's education, L. H. Powers had truly reached the end of his patience. In spite of his wife's efforts to calm him down, he exploded in a pronouncement that could be heard half-way across the town.

"Listen, young man," Les thundered. "I'd like to live in Boone. My wife would like to live in Boone. Everybody I know would like to live in Boone. But Goddamn it Nephew, everybody can't live in Boone!"

I'd like to see the government get out of war altogether and leave the whole field to private industry.
— Joseph Heller, Catch-22

Jock Head Hellums

"Gotta get some gas." Chunky grunted, flailing the steering wheel and causing the ungainly Buick Electra to suddenly veer across the wet road into the service station drive. Without the courtesy of a turn signal, as usual, he just steered across the highway perilously in front of an oncoming truck. The truck driver expressed his opinion of the maneuver with a lengthy blast of his air horn. Chunky responded by extending his left middle finger into the air, a diversion which caused the right wheels of the car to run across the end of the concrete island that separated the service station lot from the highway. The big Buick jounced crazily over the island, its rear bumper banging down hard against the concrete oval.

Fletcher [Chunky] Hellums was a good guy in most ways. He was an honest and upstanding citizen, a dedicated family man, basically the salt of the earth. But he was a major hazard on the highways: aggressive, inattentive, a chronic speeder, and one of the worst drivers I have ever known. I hated riding with him, but he always insisted on driving.

I wouldn't have been riding with him at all, but I worked for Chunky. A former high school coach and math teacher, he was now doing so well developing lake-front real estate that he offered me, his former colleague and friend, a weekend job.

Possibly due to the weather, but more likely due to his normal aversion to any physical activity, Chunky pulled the car in beside the full service pump in front of the Triangle Shell Station. The rubber hose he drove across caused a loud "ding-

ding," inside the station office, informing the attendants they had a customer. The fluorescent glare shining through the glass door from inside the service station office almost completely disappeared, as someone in an enormous olive drab parka paused in the doorway, then trotted out to the car and around to the driver's window.

Chunky lowered his window and the big parka assumed a horizontal attitude. The huge pleasant face from within the parka hood mumbled the requisite, "C'n I hep ya?" Chunky glanced up at the source of the question, did the classic double take, and thumped the steering wheel with both hands.

"Jock-head Hellums!" he practically shouted. "Where-the-hell have you been?"

He must know that guy really well, I thought. If you are going to call a man that size a name like "Jock-head," he had better be a friend of yours. Chunky was a big guy, but that service station attendant made him look small in comparison.

If ever I have seen a look of conflicted emotion on a man's face, it was at that moment. "Well, hullo Fletcher. How you doin'?" the big guy responded.

The man called Jock-head seemed moderately glad to meet up with someone he apparently once knew well. But I also thought I detected a bit of pain inflicted by the sound of a hated nickname. It was also the first time I had ever heard anyone address Chunky by his given name.

"I ain't seen you in years, man. You not in Baltimore anymore? You back home now?" Chunky obviously wanted to chat with the big guy a bit.

"Yeh, I'm back here helpin' out my Dad, I been back for several years now." A huge hand gestured towards a form behind the counter back inside the station. "My Dad bought this station near the lake, but its more than he can handle. He ain't been doin' too well lately, and I gotta' help out my dad." The gentleness and sincerity in the statement came through.

"Reg'lar or high test?" The big parka straightened up and moved purposefully toward the rear of the car, pausing with the back turned toward the open car window, and a huge hand poised above the space between the twin yellow pumps. Now Chunky had to lean out of the window and talk back toward the attendant.

"Gimme ten gallons of high test." The big hand lifted the nozzle from the premium pump and pulled the hose to the back bumper of the Buick, where the filler cap was cleverly concealed behind the license plate. The big man set the nozzle on automatic and stuffed both hands into the side pockets of his parka, but he remained near the rear of the car, with his back turned to Chunky as he watched the numbers roll up on the pump. I thought that Jock-Head Hellums, whomever he might be, was making it clear that it hadn't taken him long to see plenty of his old acquaintance.

The nozzle clunked back onto the pump and the huge form trundled up along the side of the car, stopping at arms length from the open driver's window. "That'll be four twenty-five." Chunky pulled a five out of his wallet and poked it out into the drizzle. "That's okay." He waved the attendant off as the big guy began to dig in his pocket for change. "Hey, good to see you again, man."

"Thanks Fletch. Good to see you too." The quiet, un-enthusiastic reply was blown back by the drizzle. The giant in the soggy parka trotted back to the front door of the station, momentarily interrupting the fluorescent glare as he entered.

Before we even got back onto the highway, Chunky was again thumping the steering wheel excitedly. "Hey, man! Do you know who that was?" Before I could confirm that I had no idea who he was, Chunky continued. "That was Jock-head Hellums!" Well, that much I had figured out on my own, but I assumed that Chunky knew all about the history of the man called "Jock-Head," and I was about to hear it.

"That was Maynard Hellums. You remember Maynard Hellums! He was a star offensive lineman for Southern. Me and him played together in high school. After playing out at Southern, he got drafted by the pros!" The name "Maynard Helms" seemed just the least bit familiar to me.

"Is his name Helms or Hellums?" I asked, trying to connect with the name. Is he any relation to you?

" Well, heh heh," chortled Chunky, "in Farnham County there's *Helmses* and then there's *Hellumses.* I think they were originally the same name, but if you live in town, in Claymore, the county seat, your name is probably spelled H-E-L-M-S. If you're from out in the country though, from Podunk, like Jock-head and me, you're probably a Hellums. Me and Jock-head are both from Podunk, and we are both Hellumses, but we ain't no kin, as far as I know. When we played for Farnham County High, half of the team was named either Helms or Hellums. "

"Apparently he's not playing pro ball now." I ventured.

"Naah, not for several years. Actually, I knew he wasn't still playing. Knee injuries mostly, made him way too slow. Maybe he got a concussion too. I don't think he made it but one, maybe two, seasons. He didn't get to play that much. But he was the best offensive lineman in the conference when he played at Southern, the best pulling guard in the state. He's one reason we won the conference title those two years in a row. He would open up holes in the line that I could just stroll through."

I dreaded what might be coming. Chunky was never a real star, but you would never know it by listening to him. If he ever got started telling about his glory days of football, there was nothing to do but to hunker down and endure.

"You must know that guy pretty well," I ventured. I thought that learning more about Jock-Head's story would be a great deal more interesting than hearing replays of Chunky's football exploits.

"Well, heck yeah. We went all through elementary and high school together. Well, he's a couple years older'n me, but he finished high school a year behind me. We were in the eighth and ninth grades together. He really ain't no rocket scientist." Chunky purposefully tapped his forehead.

"He probably wouldn't 'a finished high school, much less gone to college, if it hadn't been for football. Don't think he ever graduated from Southern. I'm not sure he even went to class."

"Is that why they call him Jock-Head?" That would have made sense to me.

"Naw. That's not the reason." Chunky began chuckling as he talked. "Jock-Head, uh, Maynard was already a huge kid when he first started to high school, older'n most of the kids, and everybody started telling him he ought to go out for football. We didn't have no middle school in the county, so he went out for football in the eighth grade. Of course, he could only play junior varsity in the eighth. The coach had kind of a tough time talking him into going out. I really think, as big as he was, he was actually afraid that he might hurt somebody."

"When he first went out for the team, that first August, when we were in the locker room suiting up for try outs, Maynard held up his jockey strap and asked what it was for. Then somebody asked what position he wanted to play.

'Uh, I think Coach said he was going to first try me at center,' Maynard told him.

Then the guy said to Maynard, 'Well, you get hit head-on a lot as center. When you play a line position like that, you got to wear this thing on your head to keep your helmet from rubbing your head raw.'

Everybody agreed, and then the guy told him, 'See, these two little straps here hook under your ears and the big elastic band goes under your chin, and then you put your helmet on over it, just like this.'"

Chunky pantomimed the installation of a jockey strap on his head as he drove, almost running off the road. "When we suited up, several of the guys put their supporters on their heads, just the way that guy told Maynard."

"Then somebody yelled 'Rookies go first.' We put Maynard in front, so he didn't see the other guys take the straps off their heads as we left the field house."

"We all marched out on the field, suited up in our practice uniforms, wearing our pads and everything, carrying our helmets. And there, leading the parade, was Maynard, with his jockey strap pulled down onto his head and hooked onto his ears, proud as punch."

"Well, you know what Coach Henklemeyer was like. We didn't make jokes about him being an escaped Nazi for nothing. When Coach looked over and saw Maynard, I don't think he believed what he saw. He did a big double-take and his face turned red. He went running over to Maynard and started jumping up and down and yelling at him. 'What the hell is that on your head? Have you lost your f-----g mind?'"

"Poor Maynard just looked down at Coach with this blank look like 'What's the big problem?' Then, when he looked around and saw everybody cracking up, he realized that he was the only one with his athletic supporter on his head. He knew then that he was the butt of a big joke."

"Well, everybody went home laughing about Maynard wearing his jockey strap on his head at practice, and by the time school started, everyone in town knew about it. He would have dropped out of football if Coach hadn't gone over to his house and apologized and talked him into staying. We didn't have many guys in the eighth grade that were six-foot-five and weighed two-sixty, so the coach really begged him to play."

"Coach told the rest of the team that if he ever heard any one of us call Maynard "Jock-Head" again, there would be hell to pay. But you can't stop something like that in a little town like Claymore. Off the field, everybody started calling him "Jock-Head," and the rest, as they say, is history. That's what everybody's called him ever since."

"I bet that you're the one who told him to wear his jock on his head," I accused Chunky. "That sounds to me like something you would do."

"It wasn't me! I swear to God it wasn't me!" A cackling Chunky released the steering wheel to give a protracted wave to the heavens, causing a near collision with an oncoming car. The protest served only to convince me that he was definitely the guilty party.

As the drizzle increased to a downpour, Chunky decided that driving required his full attention, and the rest of the drive back into town was spent in silence. As we rode through the rain, I felt kind of a sense of sadness, pondering what the future might hold for Maynard Hellums, the gentle giant with bad knees and a bogus education. I know what small towns are like. Once the toast of an entire state, he is now stuck back in his old home town, where he will probably live out the rest of his days, known to everyone as "Jock-Head."

Flash Dance

The instructional personnel at Peneplain Community College were well justified in declaring themselves to be overworked. Although the classroom instructors taught course loads which would have been considered unreasonable at a conventional college, it was the full-time laboratory instructors who paid the highest price for an expansion gone out of control.

No one had foreseen the exponential growth of the college's enrollment and the number of students so quickly outgrowing the facilities. The well-intended "open door" enrollment policy had resulted in the student population overwhelming the meager funding doled out by the state legislature. Still, PPCC was a community college, and the community college system was created to provide educational opportunities to those for whom a college education had previously been unavailable. It is really not surprising that the faculty agreed to carry the extra burden rather than turn students away or compromise the quality of instruction.

The greatest problem with overcrowding occurred in the school's life sciences laboratories. An economic recession had created a boom in the popularity of the allied health programs, and Human Anatomy and Physiology was a required course in every allied health program in the school. The college had only one A&P laboratory instructor, Mrs. Florence Faison, and there was no money to hire an additional one. With a few hours per week of assistance from work-study students, Mrs. Faison covered four two-hour labs a day for four days each week, with two more on sections on Friday mornings. Only Friday afternoons

remained available for the takedown and set up of the laboratory for the following week. The poor instructor even had to eat
her lunch at her desk in the laboratory most days.

Florence Faison, known to her friends as Flossie and to
her students as Mrs. Faison, was by her own admission, no bril-
liant academician, but she was certainly everything the college
administration wanted. She was a real work horse, and whatever her assignments, she always gave them her best effort.
Enthusiastic and excitable, she was demanding of her students,
but always available when they needed help. Most important,
she was unwaveringly fair in grading them. Although they occasionally did not give her the respect she deserved, most of the
students really liked her and appreciated her selfless efforts on
their behalf.

Like most college teachers, she was no slave to fashion.
She continued to wear the same huge, round eyeglasses that
had been stylish when she was a student, many years before.
Those glasses, when coupled with her natural wide-eyed facial
expression and head of thick, curly, and chronically disarrayed
hair, gave her a perpetual look of surprise. As a matter of fact,
she often was surprised. If disturbed while she was working at
her desk at the front of the lab, she might react to an unexpected
noise or salutation or touch with a startled jump and a shrill
squawk. She would often be working with her head bent down,
concentrating on paperwork, and have a student's gentle touch
and solicitous "Miz Faison?" prompt a surprised "Aaaak." This
startled response, however, was invariably followed by a warm
"What can I do to help you?"

Peneplane Community College, irreverently known as PPCC, first opened its doors in an obsolete high school building in the decaying center city of Georgetown, North Carolina. As the college expanded into the surrounding neighborhood, its location made for some interesting interactions with the residents of that part of town. When the college expanded into a building located next door to the county Substance-abuse Rehabilitation Center, clients from the center would occasionally find their way into the building, meaning that anything worth more than a nickel had to be kept under lock and key. Then, when the college opened a recreation hall for its students, hoods from the street quickly took over the pool tables. A uniformed policeman had to be stationed in the rec hall, full-time, and the presentation of a student ID made a requirement for admission. But even considering the edgy status of the neighborhood, it was a great shock when, one fine morning, a flasher appeared in the doorway of the Anatomy and Physiology Laboratory in the Granger Science and Technology Building.

The student lab coats sold in the college book store could have been designed by a flasher. Made of white cotton denim, the coats were loosely fitting and smock-like. Like most lab coats, they had a single column of large buttons down the front and huge patch pockets just below waist level on either side. If one aspired to become a flasher, all that was required was donning the lab coat, unbuttoning a few critical buttons, and holding the front of the coat closed-but-ready with hands stuffed into the patch pockets.

The flasher surely must have cased the joint in advance.

He was clever enough to realize that in the science building, no one would give someone wearing a lab coat a second glance. He also selected a laboratory room mostly occupied by young female dental hygiene students, all seated facing the wall with the doorway into the hall.

The culprit strolled, apparently unnoticed, down the side hall of the third floor of the Building. He popped in through the door of Flossie's Anatomy and Physiology lab and called out "Hey Gulls," in a loud, raspy voice. When the students (and their instructor) looked up, the flasher flipped open his lab coat. The students gasped and Mrs. Faison gave forth her famous "Aaaakkk," loud enough to be heard throughout the floor. All of this obviously gave the flasher great pleasure in the brief moment before he ducked out of the lab, ran down to the end of the hall, and disappeared into the stairwell.

Following their initial, speechless shock, the students began to mumble to one another, exchanging comments such as "Can you believe that?" or "Did you see the size of that thing." Flossie just sat at her desk, glassy-eyed and numb, finding it difficult to comprehend that her sacred A&P lab had been so crudely violated.

The episode was reported to the police, of course, and both city and campus officers responded. They interviewed several students and their instructor and gathered from the flasher's M.O. that the same individual had previously visited some other schools and hospitals in the area. But interestingly, no one could provide the authorities with an accurate description of the culprit's face. The most complete description that the police were able to assemble from the eyewitness reports was simply that the suspect was an anonymous male, of unknown age and average height, last seen wearing a white lab coat with an enormous tallywhacker protruding from the front.

As the shock wore off, the students began to treat the event with a certain amount of humor. Alluding to the cigarette lighter commercial that was continually on television about that time, they began to refer to the culprit as "the guy who flicked his Bic at Flossie." Students walking into the lab sometimes flipped their unbuttoned lab coats open in a flasher imitation. Some of Mrs. Faison's colleagues even jokingly accused her of deliberately staging the whole affair. After all, it did occur in a human anatomy and physiology lab. Mrs. Faison saw no humor what-so-ever in any of these shenanigans.

The brazen pervert continued his assault on Flossie's A&P lab, making two additional appearances that semester, each at a different time of day, but always to a lab session filled with mostly female students. But he made his big mistake when he went for a repeat performance at a lab session for a class he had visited before.

A student, arriving late for the last lab on a Thursday afternoon, scurried into the laboratory breathless and shaken. She immediately approached her instructor. "Mrs. Faison, I think that man is here again."

"That man?" Flossie did not immediately grasp to whom the student was referring.

"You know, that man. The flasher. As I was coming up the stairwell, I looked out of the window from the second floor.

I could see this guy in the parking lot getting out of his car, and as soon as he got out, he started putting on a lab coat. I think it's that man!"

"Ooooh!" Mrs. Faison's eyes grew even wider as she nodded calmly. "<u>That</u> man! Well now, you just sit down and get started on your lab. Don't say anything. Don't worry about a thing. I'll take care of this."

The student was amazed at Mrs. Faison's calm response, but she did as she was told. Flossie, however, had not simply been biding her time as she waited for the flasher to make another appearance. Plans had been laid.

The instructor momentarily disappeared into the stock room where skeletons and boxes of miscellaneous bones were kept. When she returned to the lab, Flossie was grasping a huge femur – a large human thigh bone – in her right hand. Except for the student who had alerted her, none of the students even looked up. All of the other students were completely unaware that anything out of the ordinary was going on, even as Flossie positioned herself flat against the wall beside the open door. She did not have long to wait.

"Hey Gulls," called out a raspy voice, as the man jumped through the door, simultaneously flinging open his lab coat. The instant the flasher opened his coat, Flossie pivoted around from beside door, swinging the femur downward with all her strength. The bone encountered the flasher's manhood precisely midway in its extension with a loud "Thwack." That first sound was quickly followed by an anguished "AAAAGH" voiced by the recipient of the blow.

The flasher collapsed forward to his knees, grasping for his injured manhood with one hand as he made a scrambling turn-around and crawled for the door. Flossie assisted him his exit by swinging the femur like a baseball bat and applying a sturdy whack to his buttocks. Outside in the hall, the culprit regained his footing and began his final retreat, loping with a side-ways gallop toward the stair well, clutching his groin and moaning "oooh-aah, oooh-aah," first disappearing from sight and then from hearing.

Most of the students were unaware that the flasher had even made another appearance until they heard him yell and looked up to see him making his exit by crawling out through the door. They sat frozen in dumbfounded wonder as Mrs. Faison calmly returned to her desk.

"Well then," Flossie calmly announced to the class, placing the femur on her desk and pretending to dust her hands together before wiping them on her lab coat. "I reckon one good bone deserves another."

What passes for courage is often nothing more than a lack of imagination.
— Graham Hill

Some Basic Organic Chemistry

The lovely Lucille just recently experienced the luxury of the tomato juice spa, including a full-body massage and facial. It is claimed that a mild solution of ascorbic acid, such as tomato juice, will saponify noxious oily aromatic hydrocarbons such as butyl mercaptan and miraculously convert them into benign and blessedly water-soluble compounds. This all has to do with Lucille the Bagel's (that's bagel, not beagle, but that's another story) encounter with a skunk. It was her first, and hopefully, her last such adventure.

From the moment we pulled into the drive of our mountain retreat in Mayberry on a Friday evening and Lucille leapt joyously from the car, it was clear that she was in pursuit of some nefarious creature. You should know that Lucille takes her job of protecting her territory very seriously. Whenever I pull into the drive of our home here in Charlotte, Lucille does not immediately rush up to the gate to give me her slobbery welcome. Instead, she makes a thorough patrol of the perimeter of the compound (our back yard), obviously searching for evil doers. Eventually she reports to the gate, announcing "All stations properly secured, Sir! Advance and be recognized." Then she gives me the slobbery welcome.

On weekends we often travel to the mountains, mostly to get away from the stress of city life, and Lucille always travels with us. Upon our arrival, Lucille immediately leaps from the vehicle and enthusiastically begins her patrol of the area, sniffing out interlopers, both real and imagined.

At the time of one Friday night patrol in November, the perimeter of the mountain house was obviously not secure. There most certainly was an intruder, one which Lucille promptly tracked down and subjected to her best wherewithal. Unfortunately, Lucille soon found herself on the receiving end of the intruder's own wherewithal in full measure. Having fired a single, but highly effective salvo, the skunk retreated into a rhododendron thicket leaving Lucille temporarily incapacitated. First she groveled along on the ground, pushing her face through the leaves, snorting and barfing. She then rolled around on the ground for a few minutes before making her miraculous recovery and loping gleefully back to her masters. She proudly proclaimed, "There! I've saved the place again!" and was totally befuddled to find her efforts so unappreciated. Her masters scurried into the house to figure out what to do next, leaving a confused Lucille abandoned to the cold and dark.

We were not totally without resources. My cousin, who lives in the same area of the mountains, has always kept dogs. She has a Black Labrador Retriever who liaisons with a woods kitty regularly on a bi-annual basis. (The cousin has concluded that Black Labs have a six-month memory span, which if true, puts them above about fifty percent of the human population.) Anyway, at some point I had heard my cousin describe how she and her husband had used tomato juice to remove skunk oil from the fur of her unfortunate canine and then rinsed him off in the creek.

A quick trip to the local general store provided us with four giant-sized cans of low-grade tomato juice, but with the temperature approaching the low 20's, the creek was rejected as an appropriate site for the decontamination. The basement shower stall was agreed upon as the next best location, all towels deemed ratty enough to be sacrificed were collected, and the process was underway.

Let me make it clear that Lucille is a good dog. She is amazingly cooperative, even when being bathed, with one exception. I am not sure that she or any other dog can control this reflex, but as soon as she becomes thoroughly soaked, she gives fourth her tremendous tip-of-the-nose to the tip-of-the-tail, ear-flopping, eye-popping, tail-flailing, shake! Lucille is half basset hound, so she has plenty of excess skin, all of which she can instantly rev up to her resonant frequency, spreading an intense curtain of droplets over a radius of several meters. This is pretty ordinary dog behavior, I know, but this particular time, Lucille's hide was saturated with tomato juice!

With the application of a gallon and a half of tomato juice (the shower stall looked like it belonged to Norman Bates), followed by two vigorous soapings with pine-scented doggie shampoo, we thought that Lucille was well on her way back to being her old, fragrant self. Unfortunately, she still had too much butyl mercaptan residue stubbornly clinging to her fur to be tolerated in the house, even in the basement. An uncomprehending Lucille was banished for the weekend to the tool shed, normally her summer quarters.

By Saturday morning our sense of smell had recovered enough for even a short visit from Lucille to reveal that the tomato juice had not worked nearly as well as we had first thought. We called my cousin, the skunk spray removal expert, in a panic. "Oh yes," she confessed. "We have decided that tomato juice really does not work all that well." She went on to describe how she had recently found that a mixture of hydrogen peroxide, baking soda, and dish-washing detergent worked much better.

Fortunately, the general store had a couple of bottles of hydrogen peroxide in stock, and I bought them both. The clerk behind the counter was the same lady from whom I had purchased the tomato juice the previous evening. "You folks must be having a serious skunk problem," she sagely observed. I was impressed with her powers of observation, until I realized that it was probably just my smell, rather than any deduction based on my purchases that prompted her comment.

But tomato juice, peroxide, baking soda, detergent, cedar shavings, and time can work wonders. We were able to return to Charlotte on Sunday with only minor distress and the most obvious long-term effect being that Lucille is now a blond.

If you happened to have been on I-77 that Sunday afternoon, you might have noticed a vintage green Explorer headed South with a dog inside and the people hanging out of the windows, instead of the other way around. But we, including the dog, all survived and are now returning to what, for us, is considered normal. So far as I am concerned, the incident is ended, or at least it will be once I can convince my wife that red polka-dotted bathroom walls are actually rather attractive.

A man who carries a cat by the tail learns something he can learn in no other way.

— Mark Twain

Bri Wink

Although I was not there for the actual birthing, I should be numbered among those stalwart souls who nurtured Peneplane Community College through its adolescent angst. The community college system in North Carolina was only a few years old when I went to work there. Although the college's administrators maintained a facade of boundless confidence, it sometimes appeared they might be feeling their way through this new kind of institution of higher education, learning mostly through trial and error.

The administration initially professed some patently democratic ideals about education, as manifested through such liberal policies as "the open door" (no admission requirements other than a high school diploma), the students' "right to fail" (no enforced prerequisites), a "non-punitive grading system" (Incomplete's instead of D's or F's), and the mantra that "Given enough time, any student can successfully complete [almost] any educational task." Some of those innovations worked pretty well and some did not work at all.

In the beginning, the "open door" at the college was a good political decision. From the day it first opened its doors, the school attracted an unanticipated number of enrollees. In order to manage the extraordinarily large number of first-time students at PPCC efficiently, the usual requirements for admission such as testing, counseling, and pre-registration were largely dispensed with. The early-model IBM computer in the data processing center was overwhelmed by student data, meaning that no official class rosters were available at the beginning of the term. The initial class rosters were obtained by the instructor passing a legal pad around the room at the first class meeting to collect names and social security numbers.

After only a couple of years of existence, the college's booming enrollment meant that almost every instructor was required to teach more than the normal load. Instructors were also sometimes required to teach courses far outside of their field of training. Policies such as these were in effect the fall term that Physics 5401 - Shop Science I, was added to my already burdensome load of conventional physics courses. Now, I'm no academic snob, and I never objected to teaching vocational-level courses. In my opinion, anyone can teach physics to a class full of rocket scientists, but teaching physics to people who have spent years avoiding mathematics requires a special talent. This "Shop Science" course was the only formal exposure to physics most of these folks were ever going to have. I held the conviction that physics was especially important for students in areas such as automotive mechanics, welding, or respiratory therapy, so I always gave it my best effort.

In the initial class meeting of PHY 5401, Section 1, the yellow legal pad had already made its first round of the classroom. I was just beginning my pep talk on what the class was all about and how useful it could be, when in walked – no, in sprang – an amazing and intimidating figure. One of the first things noticeable about this well-over-six-feet, one hundred and twenty pound individual was that he did not simply walk from one point to another. Every movement he made was exceedingly quick and exaggerated. His head was topped by such a caboodle of tousled hair, it appeared that he might tip over at any moment. I estimated that his steps were about eight feet long; I could tell because he went from the door at the front of the room to a desk in the opposite back corner in about half a dozen quick springs. Once there, he selected the corner desk, folded into it like a collapsing tent, and instantly went sound asleep.

I walked back, yellow legal pad in hand, and stood beside the desk he had just occupied. "And what is your name, sir?" I intentionally asked the question much more loudly than necessary. His head jolted erect and his eyes clicked wide open.

"Bri wink," I thought I heard him say.

"How's that?" I wanted to be sure.

"Bri Wink," he confirmed.

I didn't want to spend class time making an issue of his name, so I simply presented him with the roster pad. "Would you please sign in?" I requested. "We need your full name and your social security number."

Mr. Wink dutifully patted himself down in search of a writing implement before finally accepting the ball point pen I presented to him. He then went through an extensive routine of arm stretching and finger flexing before hunkering over and applying himself to the task. He bent studiously over the pad, tongue firmly clenched in the corner of his mouth, inscribing a line of characters across the bottom of the page which could have been in the Vulcan alphabet, so far as I could tell.

"I need for you to print your name." I instructed.

"That is printin'," he informed me. "I can't write writin'."

Upon closer inspection, the combination of upper case Roman and lower case cursive characters spelled out something that did somewhat resemble Bri Wink. So Bri Wink he would be, at least until the official roster came out. As long as he answered to "Mr. Wink" when the roll was called, there would be no problem.

As we left the room at the end of class, I encountered my friend John Smith, instructor of mathematics and chairman of the department to which the vocational physics courses had recently been assigned.

"I see you have Bri Wink in your class," he observed.

"So it would appear. Do you know anything about him? Is that really his name?" I saw this as my chance to clear up some of the confusion.

"He was in my Shop Math class this morning," John revealed, "but he slept through most of the class. I guess Bri Wink must really be his name; that's what I thought I heard him say, and I think that's sort of what it looked like on the roster." Three weeks later, when we did obtain the official printed class roster, we learned that it was one Bryson Winkler who had matriculated for Shop Science, Shop Math, and some automotive-repair technology courses. But by this time, Bri Wink was indelibly planted in all our brains.

The head of the Automotive Technology Program, Claude Hunter, also had Bri Wink in his class. Some weeks into the term, while conferring over lunch about our students-in-common, we shared the observation that Mr. Wink appeared to have some difficulty reading. Everyone had noticed, however, that he was clever and resourceful in solving practical math problems. He showed up, usually tardy, for every class, and he always fell asleep shortly after his arrival. Claude thought that Bri possibly had the potential to become a really good mechanic, if only he could be taught to read the shop manuals. Claude, who always took a strong personal interest in his automotive mechanics students, had also learned that Bri commuted a considerable distance to PPCC and worked nights to support himself and several siblings.

Becoming more aware of Mr. Wink's personal situation made us more tolerant of his sleeping in class, but it actually was not his snoozing that made him such a legend. His main claim to fame was his instantly switching from sound asleep to full awake in the middle of an instructor's presentation and immediately waving frantically to get the instructor's attention. Once acknowledged by the instructor, he would usually present the instructor with a question totally unrelated to the topic at hand.

One day, after dozing through the first half of John Smith's math class, he suddenly came to full alert and began waving his hand frantically.

"Mister Smif! Mister Smif!" he implored.

John was encouraged. "Bri has a math question," He thought. "Yes, Mr. Wink?"

"Mister Smif, did you know that the little end of your necktie is a whole lot longer than the big end?" That was Mr.

Wink's sincere concern.

In my shop science class one day, during an electricity demonstration he abruptly awoke and began the hand waving for which he was becoming famous.

"Doctor Max?" he asked. "How, does a dam make 'lectwicty?"

At least we were studying electricity that day, unlike the day when out, of the blue, he presented me with the conundrum, "Dr. Max, I know where mules come from. That's a cross between a jackass and a mare. But where do they get jackasses from?" I bit my tongue.

In automotive shop one day, Bri interrupted near the end of a detailed explanation of the automotive electrical system to complain that he simply did not understand Mr. Hunter's explanation. Claude, the most patient of instructors, repeated his entire explanation, from battery to spark plugs, this time more slowly and in more detail, dedicating most of the remaining class time to Mr. Wink's question.

Bri paid rapt attention to every word, but the detailed explanation remained far from satisfactory. Bri complained, "Aw, Mr. Hunter, I know all that. But whar does the fahr come from?"

In shop science laboratory, since Bryson had difficulty comprehending the written lab instructions, he would stand back from the table and let his lab partners follow the written instructions and perform the actual manipulations. Electronic calculators had just become available at an affordable price, and Bri was one of the first in his shop science class to own one.

Throughout the laboratory session, Bri would stand, holding his calculator at ready, should anyone need anything calculated. How he loved to use that calculator! If anyone, anywhere in the lab, needed a volume or a torque or a viscosity calculated, they only needed to call out the data. Bri would make the calculation in a flash, and it was almost always correct.

The unfortunate part of the story is that Mr. Winkler did not successfully complete a single class his first term at PPCC, or the next. The much better part of the story is that, when provided with some competent counseling, he took what he was told to heart and took the recommended remedial reading and communications courses. Sometime in the third year of our acquaintance, he successfully completed shop science, and for several terms after that I would occasionally see him on campus. I was always greeted with a cheerful "Hey Doctor Max," and an exuberant wave.

Eventually though, as the student population continued to grow and the automotive program was moved to another part of the campus, Bri Wink dropped off our radar screens. But he most certainly was not forgotten.

For several years after our former department head, John Smith, had moved to greener pastures in Raleigh, he would call me up whenever he had some gossip to share about the shenanigans in the Department of Community Colleges. When I would answer the phone, John would invariably greet me with "Hey Mac, how's Bri Wink doing these days?" Unfortunately, I would always have to respond that I really didn't know. After not getting any calls from John for a long period of time, I called his office in Raleigh and learned that he had tragically died in an automobile accident.

Claude Hunter became a nationally recognized authority in automotive mechanics training, serving as a consultant to community colleges from North Carolina to California. One of his most popular presentations was titled "Where Does the Fire Come From?" Instructors were then advised that they should not spend a lot of time providing students with a detailed answer until they were sure they had understood the students' question.

Time and budget constraints proved many of the more idealistic policies at PPCC to be impractical, and by the late eighties, most of the more innovative policies, such as the open door and non-punitive grading, had been abandoned. Along with more conventional methods of educational management and pedagogy, some of the trappings of traditional higher education were adopted. These trappings included a full-dress graduation ceremony, something which became an exercise in endurance and a caricature of academic tradition over the years. Several hundred students actually walk across the stage to receive their diplomas in the PPCC graduation ceremony now, a process that literally takes hours. The event is held in the Old Charlotte Coliseum, a location which appears to have led the families of some of the first-generation community college graduates to conclude that, just like Smack-Down Wrasslin' (held in the same facility), audience participation is obligatory. (The conferral of Billy Bob's degree at the graduation ceremony is likely to be accompanied by a chorus of "Yee Haw,

Billy Bob! Way to go! Wahoo!") My strategy for coping with this graduation-a-thon was to have a glass of wine before leaving home and perhaps use the conferral of degrees procession as an opportunity for a good nap.

A few years ago during the ceremony, I was comfortably dozing, just vaguely aware of the voice announcing that this student or the other was receiving his or her Diploma or Degree in whatever. But then the voice reading the names of the recipients penetrated my psyche, and I was propelled into consciousness.

"Bryson Winkler," the voice resonated and paused. I waited, fully expecting to hear "Junior," but the word never came; I heard instead, "Associate of Applied Science, Automotive Technology." When I was able to focus my eyes on the stage, there he was! A little grizzled and worn like me, but it was him alright, springing across the stage with strides eight feet long and thirty years deep. "Bryson Winkler, Associate of Applied Science!" I was astounded and delighted.

I rarely attended the student reception following graduation, but this time I had to see if I could find Mr. Winkler. I searched the long lines queued up at the tables of punch and sandwiches, but he spotted me first. "Doctor Max, Doctor Max," he yelled, frantically waving his famous wave. He came pouncing across the floor and pumped my hand enthusiastically. He then grabbed me by the shoulders and propelled me over to the edge of the crowd where he introduced me to his proudly smiling wife as "his favorite teacher at PPCC," adding that he learned more useful stuff in physics than in any other class.

That could have been because it took three tries for him to complete it, but coming some thirty years after the fact, I considered it the greatest affirmation of my chosen career that I had ever experienced.

Bryson explained to me that he had been operating a successful automobile repair business for many years now, and just a couple of years before, he had decided to return to school to complete his Associate in Applied Science Degree.

"I just wanted to get the degree for my personal satisfaction," he told me.

Hearing Bri Wink describing the completion of his degree using the phrase "for my personal satisfaction" is one of the strongest recommendations for our community colleges I have ever heard and I concluded that Bri Wink is a true embodiment of what community colleges are all about. First and foremost, the job of any college is to provide training to help people earn their daily bread and improve the quality of their lives. But job number two is helping those people also achieve their own "personal satisfaction."

It is always sad when one loses a friend, but driving home after that graduation ceremony, I felt more sadness over the death of my friend and former boss, John Smith, than at any time since his untimely demise. If I could only have given John a call, when he answered the phone, I surely would have greeted him with "Well John, let me tell you about Bri Wink. He is doing just fine."

Every man is enthusiastic at times. One man has enthusiasm for thirty minutes, another man has it for thirty days. But it is the man who has it for thirty years who makes a success in life.

— Edward B. Butler